WHAT IS We TO YOU?!

LARRY ODELL JOHNSON

Inks and Bindings
888-290-5218
www.inksandbindings.com
orders@inksandbindings.com

CONTENTS

INTRODUCTION

I have discovered that for certain kinds of academic communication, it is impractical to use the formal or traditional style of writing to convey information. Using multiple quotes from various sources and making the requisite citations to grant use of the statements of others is a technique designed to help one explain—by way of description and explanation or by comparison and justification—what one is attempting to say. This approach is what is typical of academic-styled literature. However, that is not what this treatise will do. I am going to use an autobiographical and narrative style to introduce what I have chosen to illustrate in this project. I will not use many quotations and reserve my citations. In the second and critical final chapter of this treatise, I will more readily use a *keyed cipher* to provide a *content analysis* of some limited scriptural text. To wit, items limited primarily to the first four chapters of the book of Genesis, in the King James Version (KJV) of the Holy Scriptures. Being aware that the Scriptures use a variety of techniques to convey its messages, I decided to investigate what had been my long-standing curiosity about a segment of what has traditionally been represented to me—in the Scriptures—by numerous scriptural pundits, a.k.a. preachers. Consequently, there will be some surprises forthcoming. Bottom line, I am simply seeking a fair representation of the proximate textural truth of what scriptural scholars have translated and not mere popular hearsay or other people's opinions. I decided that if grown folk cannot tell me a simple truth, then I am obliged to discover it for myself, now that I have developed skills of my own. The notion that mankind was condemned to sin because two people ate an apple from a tree never even passed the laugh test with me. However, on the spiritual side, I have always viewed the Scriptures for what I believe they are overall: our moral compass as used together with the proven fair laws which govern society. Yet while accepting these ideas—in the spirit of George Santayana—on *animal faith,* I have maintained a healthy degree of *skepticism* with respect to those who feign absolute and literal certainty regarding the immediate content in scriptural text.

In what follows, I will ease you into a process of *content analysis* using a key-cipher that I have developed over years of study. Within the narrative, I will randomly select words and phrases—which you will observe to be underlined and then immediately followed by *"bracketed"* comments—the ciphered content. Occasionally, I will repeat the process within the brackets themselves using *braces or parentheses* as interior grouping symbols. I will use these additional grouping symbols in the same way that I use the brackets to extend the immediate content, commentary, and meanings. Thus, they will act as punctuation marks when needed, and each will be appropriately "opened" and "closed." Although I will not systematically define my key or other necessary techniques used, I will demonstrate their revelations by way of their application in punctuated textual materials. In other words, you will be obliged to *beg the question* (a.k.a. take my word for it)—with respect to the meanings—as the narrative will unfold. In the end, I will use my key to unpack portions of what is revealed in the early chapters of Genesis as <u>delineated</u> [educated eat end do lie] interpretations. Additionally, I should note that when I use the word "or" and the forward-slash symbol / (solidus; oblique) for the word "or," I will mean the "inclusive" sense. That is, either-or, or both, as contrasted with the "exclusive" sense meaning simply either-or.

My goal here is to arrive at some unbiased objective truths about scriptural content and—at the same time—not proselytize. I do not need to tell people how to behave. However, I do believe that a more complete and fair set of facts will potentially aid them in their choices. When I am done, the Scriptures should assuredly remain our guide to a moral compass, and one will likely have greater insight to work with.

I will begin this narrative by introducing you to the earliest years of my life, yielding a few biographical facts about myself, while providing a sampling of the random content expanding *revelatory* technique mentioned and exampled earlier in this introduction. On this point, my approach is to position my style on the side of C.G. Jung's psychology as the "disinterested observer." A position that Sigmund Freud—the moralist—denied was possible and which caused and defined the socio-political rift between these two giants in the studies of psychology. Consequently, I will be able to provide you with a demonstration of semiotics and hermeneutics without dragging our heads through the murkier waters of these studies.

CHAPTER ONE

SEX WIT ALREADY MADE (MATRIX)

I was born in Harlem, New York. In fact, I was born in Harlem Hospital and—I am told—either on a gurney in a hallway or on a gurney in an elevator. In either case, I never made it to the birth room. No matter, I am here born to wonderful parents and surrounded by multiple caring aunts and uncles. My parents and I lived in a multi-family tenement building in the middle of the fourteen hundred blocks of Amsterdam Avenue in Harlem: along with the families of one of my mom's four sisters and three of my mom's six brothers, their spouses, and their kids. I remember the building in vivid ways. It was heated by a coal furnish that a "super" (superintendent) controlled in the large cellar. A coal truck would pull up and deliver the coal through a double-sided set of sidewalks leveled metal doors, down a metal slide onto a smaller pile on the cellar floor. As needed, the _super_ [are we people you seen] would shovel coal into the large fiery furnace down there. There were three or four floors of apartments, where individual apartments at opposite ends of the landings were separated in the center by the shared lone hallway toilet. To the right of the lone entrance and exit to each apartment was a very large and wide countertop beneath that doubled as the apartment bathtub and counter space (in our case, a counter for my parents to cut out patterns when tailoring new clothing). The entrance/exit door had one of those steel bar locks, where one end of the bar was inserted into a metal brace secured in the wooden floor and the other end inserted into the metal lock attached to the door. The type of locking mechanism that made it virtually impossible for

1

someone to force the door open from the outside. One would enter the apartment into the kitchen/bathtub area moving through a doorless entrance to the first bedroom and then through a second doorless entrance to a second bedroom/living room. When you entered the building on the ground floor, you had to walk at least, I would guess, twenty-five feet to the staircase that led to the first level of apartments. The cellar door was to the rear and beneath that ground-level staircase. To me that is where the scary "super" man lived, under the long dark hallway staircase. I recall having to enter the hallway by myself once when the super deliberately scared me as my dad sat outside on the sidewalk. When I came back outside, I told my dad what the super had done, and he immediately went and spoke to the super. It never happened again! He is fortunate that I only spoke to my dad. Had I told my teenaged male cousins, he might have been in some serious trouble, because they were kind of tough and very protective of me.

Unlike one of my mom's brother's wives, my mom kept the roach problem under control in our apartment. That aunt, who lived in our building, never appeared bothered by all the roaches that ran unchallenged around everywhere in her apartment. Her roach problem was so bad that one day when she sprayed while my sister and I were standing in her _kitchen_ [enter we itch okay], she had to light some old newspaper on fire to quell all the roaches that started literally flying around in her kitchen. (I would be willing to bet that you did not know that German roaches could fly.) It was a nasty and frightening situation! My sister and I had to go outside her apartment and into the hallway until the roaches calmed down. I am sure that she sprayed in front of us trying to leave the impression that she really did try to control the roach problem in her house, but the reaction of the roaches to that little bit of spraying exposed the _lie_. What was odd about her was that she seemed kind but <u>docile</u> [we _lack . . . I see do_]. I only recall one other very brief time ever reentering her apartment, along with my mom, and I stood in one spot in the middle of the floor anxious to leave.

Separately, I recall my dad's frustrated efforts to keep large rats from periodically getting into our kitchen. He would be stuffing mesh wire around pipes and placing metal pipe fittings over that; still rats would occasionally get in. My sister and I slept in the first bedroom off from the kitchen, and we would hear my dad scramble through our space into the kitchen to use a straw broom to kill a large rat. And he was good at it! After some commotion, he would often show us his dead prey to assure us we were safe. As for my mom, if she ever heard or even heard of a rat, we kids would have to fend for ourselves. I also recall that my mom was so afraid of caterpillars that she would not sleep on sheets with butterfly images on them. I know because, as an adult and awaiting a visit from my mom during a time when I was living in LA, I spent some decent money, at the Beverly Center in Beverly Hills, California, on some beautiful butterfly patterned _designer_ [new game is we do / hour we sign . . . we do!] sheets for her, all for naught.

My relatives were a major presence on our block. Of course, there was also the really mean lady who used to always yell profanely out her window to the oldest one of her sons to summon him home. He was always only allowed to stay outside ten to fifteen minutes max. She would yell what sounded like, "George Raff," get your so-and-so expletive back in this house. And she would beat him a lot. He eventually ran away from home. The next time I saw him years later, he was the actor John Brown who starred as the janitor on the TV sitcom _Good Times_. Speaking of actors, my mom's friend Mantan Moreland of the Charlie Chan detective movies would visit us. He once bought all the kids on our block large Harmon harmonicas in purple velvet-lined boxes. As a little kid, it was just another toy to me, as opposed to an actual professional instrument. And neither of my parents made me the wiser. The last time that I recall seeing it, the metal sidings had been carefully removed by me and only the wooden framework was showing.

My mom would tell me about all the famous celebrities that she knew, met, or had seen while living in Harlem before I was born. Which brings me to a story of theoretical significance that my mom related to me, and I several times overheard her relate to others, about my reaction to a groin hernia surgery that I had when I was two years old. As my mom consistently related the story, I refused to utter a single word when spoken to on my way home from my surgery and hospital stay. This was apparently atypical of me, as I was somewhat gregarious for my age I am told. However, we are told that as soon as I was comfortably home, I blurted out, "Mommy, the doctor cut my *wee-wee* off!" The concept of a "wee-wee" will play an important role in the theoretical construct that I am unfolding, building, and will explain within this narrative.

Amsterdam Avenue was always teeming with activity. Many different and sometimes strange faces constantly walking past in both directions during good weather, and my numerous family members always sitting in chairs and doing things like drinking beer and chatting outside during those good weather times. Quiet as it is kept, some of my family members would be out there in all types of weather. My mom told me that my dad supported us in those days by selling flavored shaved ice during the warm months (I recall the silver rectangular metal shaver with the little door that would fill up with ice, the cone-shaped cups, and the large block of ice he would shave from, doubtless I ate my share of those Icey's), and he would run the numbers [*seen are we . . . be man . . . you then run*] at other times. In the interim, as a veteran, my dad was taking advantage of G.I. Bill to finance his learning tailoring [*game win outlook . . . I all that*]. I was also told that my dad was even a whiskey runner [*new run key his way*] in his youth. With reference to that, I once saw a photo of my dad in his youth wearing a holstered gun, holding a rifle, and wearing a cowboy-type hat. It reminded me of the iconic Billy the Kid photo. The photo has since disappeared, and when I asked my dad about it as an adult, he denied it ever existed.

4

My older sister and only sibling possessed the photo last, so I can only imagine what she could have done with it.

I first learned to distinguish a person's physical color differences as a toddler. My dad's youngest brother who had green eyes was a merchant marine, who began dating and eventually marrying for life one of the light-skinned or "high yellow" twin sisters that lived in the building next to the funeral home at the end of our block. Their beauty and skin tone stood out from others of us. Then there was the definitive time when two of my teenaged male cousins, each holding one of my hands, ran me around the corner by the funeral home and proceeded to grab one of the white teenagers from around the corner. They held him down on the ground and directed me to smack him in the face several times. Then calmly let him up and told him to leave. Thereafter they both squatted down, looked me in the face, and emphatically said, "Never be afraid of white people!" And I never have been! Nor have I developed the habit of mind of just generally disliking, *fearing,* or *even hating* white people, like I feel too many undereducated Black people seem obliged to waste their spiritual energy doing.

My immediate family was the first to move from Amsterdam Avenue when I was around three or four years old, followed a few months later by my mom's sister who had an apartment in the building. We would often return to visit my mom's siblings who remained there. Our two families moved to the Fort Greene-Farragut area of Brooklyn at the base of the Brooklyn Bridge. My immediate family lived at 233 Sand Street across the street from the main entrance of the Brooklyn Navy Yard and my aunt lived at Nine Monument Walk in Fort Greene. Later on, one of my uncles moved to a building in Fort Greene on the Cumberland Hospital side of the projects. My immediate family moved because my dad had secured a job at the Navy Yard. He had only to walk across the street to enter the Yard. We lived on the twelfth floor, and I loved the apartment. My sister and I both had our separate rooms, there were no rats or roaches, and we could see great distances from our windows. There was a full bathroom and full kitchen in the apartment, and an incinerator door in the hallway outside the apartment from which to dispose of garbage. There was also a laundromat in the basement of a nearby building where Mom could easily wash and dry our clothes. Even though I had gotten used to the routines of living in Harlem, having to share the toilet in the hallway outside our apartment with other families and the killing of rats, I did not miss Amsterdam Avenue at all.

I recall four major occasions when we returned to visit Amsterdam Avenue. Once my maternal grandfather drove up from his wonderful farm in South Carolina to visit his kids, my aunts and uncles. One day during that several days of his visit, I witnessed my grandad beat three of his sons in a brief footrace. Each summer my immediate family would spend time at my grandad's farm during my dad's yearly summer vacation. During that round trip, we would also spend some days visiting my fraternal grandmother and my dad's oldest brother in Louisiana and my dad's older sister in <u>Chicago</u> [offer game already *see I hear sees*]. I enjoyed leaving New York on these road trips and visiting with my grandparents and other relatives on both sides of the family. However, the dread was my dad's attitude about having to stop for rest area breaks other than refueling. Once we were back in the car, he would invariably announce that we were not going to stop again for any reason before some outrageously long period. Every time he did that, and he would unwaveringly say it, I would immediately feel like I had the urge to go again or would endure the fear of having to go in the interim periods between stops. As a child, I grew to resent him for that. However, as an adult I clearly understand why he had to put that kind of pressure on us. We were traveling through the Jim Crow South and there were no hotels that would rent us space to stay over. So he wanted to reach certain locations along the roadway before we were forced to sleep in our car on the side of the road. When that happened, Mom—who was not a smoker—would stay awake and puff cigarette smoke over us to help reduce mosquito bites; there was no air conditioning in cars we rode in back then.

Another visit to the avenue was on the occasion of the grand opening of a fish and chips restaurant that one of my cousins opened in a building next door on the block. Yet another occasion was to console one of my uncles whose wife had taken a fatal fall from a window in their apartment. Lastly, there was the occasion when my mom received a phone call urging her to get to Amsterdam Avenue immediately. The police had one of her brothers, George, in handcuffs outside the building and there was a dead body on the sidewalk in front of the building. Everyone in the family was assuming the worst. Albeit the shortest of all the brothers, he was by far the toughest. Gentle demeanor but gangster tough! He was the same uncle whose wife had fallen to her death, and he had previously been a prize fighter and a mortician. We were there for hours on a cold winter's evening, before they eventually released my uncle. Still the body remained on the sidewalk for a longer time. Apparently, the city morgue was full. They eventually removed the body to a fire escape at a police station until a coroner would take possession, you cannot make these things up. What had happened to my uncle is that he was standing outside our building when he surprised an old friend, who had happened to be passing by. They embraced each other and the man died in his arms. Like I said, you cannot make these things up.

As other memories of activities on the avenue fade, like my mom using a washboard to wash cloths, the old man that lived above the funeral home missing us kids with the hot water he would toss out trying to chase us kids away from making noise under his window, diaper and milk deliveries made to our door, and Justine "Baby" Washington hanging around our building with her best friend, my cousin Laura. The two of them had previously been members of a successful singing group. My cousin had been the lead singer of the group. When she married, her husband no longer wanted her to travel with the group, so the group disbanded, and Baby Washington became a moderately successful solo artist. In thinking of my cousin Laura and her wonderful voice, I am doubly reminded of just how tough my family can be at times. I recall that on one occasional visit back to Amsterdam, my cousin Laura got into a heated argument and then an actual fistfight with her husband, on the street, while several of my relatives initially stood back. Had her husband asked me, I would have forewarned him that she had some tomboyishness in her. Too late, she beat him with fist punches like a grown man. She gave him one of those "You ruined my career, and you have the nerve to talk shit ass whippings," before my other relatives could step in to rescue him. Mind you, he tried to punch back, but she had skills.

Living in Brooklyn was a whole new world. There was plenty of room in the apartment to play and plenty of new kids outside to get to know and play with, in grassy and sandy areas. Nursery school began and I hated it, because I was separated from my mom for the first time and for all day. The only redeeming feature of nursery school was lunch and the Fig Newton or Davy Crockett cookies they would serve with milk for a snack in the afternoon. Mom had begun working as a seamstress at times or house cleaner. And each day when she came to pick me up, sometimes late, seemed like a new beginning for me. There was a black-and-white TV in our home by then, with various shows to watch like Westerns, Superman, Flash Gordon, Howdy Doody, Mickey Mouse Club, the Andy Devine Show, Amos and Andy, Popeye the Sailor Man, Road Runner, Felix the Cat, Roy Rodgers, Lassie, Rin Tin-Tin, the Lone Ranger, Davy Crockett, Bugs Bunny, the Little Rascals, Soupy Sales, and other fun things to watch. _Of course_ [cures out find out], the Soupy Sales show predated _Sesame Street_ [street same we scene]. _Soupy Sales_ [sales why soup] was a controversial kids show where the host would repeatedly be sanctioned for making sexual innuendos. For example, he once said, _"My wife can't cook, but she sure knows how_ *to make my banana cream."* Outside there were marbles and bottle top games to be played, swings to swing on, monkey bars to be climbed, and German luger-styled water guns to fill and shoot.

Looking back, I can see what the avenue had imprinted into my psyche [*we hear see women sense penis / he sees why sense pages*]. I use this term *psyche* within the context defined by C.G. Jung. The spoken words on the avenue had made me conscious of the concepts of work, women, sex, and beauty. What I observed in the activities on the avenue had made my "psyche" conscious of the concepts of color and hue. I understood the difference between Black people and White people with respect to the natural yet still amorphous differences. I could see the variety of contrasting hues of Black people and sensed the favored shades. Very early in my thoughts, it was obvious to me that people in general had a natural affinity toward and showed a great deal of favoritism toward people who were naturally pretty and people who had the fairest skin tone pigmentation, the lightest, and most of all, white skin color. I experienced this through direct observation, and I understand it today within C.G. Jungian psychology as an *archetype* [*we penises women touch . . . he sees our areas* / type . . . *he sees hours/ours already*]. Something Jung says is a primitive mental image inherited from our earliest cultural ancestors and that forever remains present in our collective subconscious. There exists a natural affinity of sexual desire for women from men, so women of all colors feel and exhibit a haughtiness toward men. How to control men, use *stealth* [steal thoughts]?! While *haughtiness* [senses seen we in *hit* game you already had] is the by-product of this degree of favoritism. Those naturally in possession of these positive biological assets are understandably *challenged* to be humble. This should be plainly obvious and readily understood by any adult, who does not let opinion and bias blind them to objective truth. It is a perfectly natural human reaction to being highly favored as compared to those who are less favored or even not favored at all, *"persona non grata"* [before already {why read look around} ours got no into a no-sense pew]. And since it is a women's physical attributes which are the most prized in a male-dominated cultural environment, we can understand why Jung could explain how haughtiness would eventually result in the "animus" [some you mean I *enters* all] we see projected from women, as evidenced in the cattiness that many women display toward each other; and especially, among certain cultural groups toward darker-skinned people. It is all part of a cultural standard, subtly promoted in media corpses [press over sees] and everyday exhibitions of respective genders "cheese caking" and "beef caking" within cultural groups. It is a psychological continuum most notably exhibited in "High Fashion" [*No, I heard . . . since areas fine . . . heed give I head*], and as an historically ubiquitous [*sin you offered quit . . . I be you*] practice. This speaks to what I call the "Aryan Syndrome" [me over hours do enter women scene any hours always]. These emotions are not confined to color alone. So one might ask what might be the solution?! I call it *"color concurrence."* First seeing and accepting the obvious, and then constructing a personal outlook and behavioral action plan that *supersedes* the obstacles to emotional growth and success imposed on the individual by these most obvious handicaps. Which is a remedy and yet not a cure! That is, it imposes on the individual the responsibility of shielding themselves from these types of social and cultural biases.

During my youth, Brooklyn introduced me to a much more expanded world. There was Kindergarten [get near ours we kind] (I still have my kindergarten diploma my mom had preserved for me), elementary school (P.S. 287), first grade, second grade, and so on. There were people of all shades and colors off to work and returning from work every day on the elevators [ours open after feels] in our building. Outside there were Marines and sailors from around the world entering and exiting the Naval Yard. Also living in the area were Puerto Ricans, Italians, West Indians and East Indians, a few Asians, Jehovah's Witnesses constantly coming to our apartment door and ringing our bell (given that the original Watchtower building—even before they connected the two former factory buildings—was right up the street on Sand Street), and mostly "kind" white schoolteachers.

Consequently, my psyche was introduced to the concepts of "the rat race" [we see all hours after hours he thinks] and "ethnicity" [city in we thoughts/women "it" sees end we hit / why it sees in . . . he thinks]. So "race" as I fundamentally [women all tell men fun already done / ally told men indict fun] understood it then, and in a more enlightened way understand it now, has always been the competition between groups of people over who first masters or controls all forms of work activity known to man and needed by man, that is, necessary to the survival of mankind, as a "group goal," and by the numbers. Therefore "race" as "racism" is simply "discrimination" [in out I after entering I mind . . . I our science ideas / nation I mean. I our science ideas]. A modern-day stratagem of using color as a rationale and justification to disguise the reality of the incessant generational birth cohort competition for jobs between designated groups, and the devious tactics used to block fair opportunities to groups marginalized by color alone, developing practical work dominance as power. This complex of socially negative behaviors and activities that help to structure and maintain this necessary and sufficient edifice of discrimination is better known to sociology as social structure. Left unchecked insidious [sense you offered idea . . . I sin / us offer ideas I sense in I] social structure can become an archetype. Thus, "I do"—the diamond ring [give in ours do no mind already idea]—thus marriage has become the symbolic representation and measurement of the relative socioeconomic and psychological strength of social groups. Viewed from this perspective, racism is not personal it is a business, a means to an end. That end is to achieve "prosperity" [why target I (to) prosper] by any means necessary and at the expense of a politically targeted social group.

11

In Brooklyn, the variety of beautiful people that I was surrounded by was palpable. There was Yvonne C. on the fourth floor, Pamela on another floor, Beatrice and her beautiful West Indian sisters on the first floor, and Betty T. in the building across the street, #234. My mom and dad had met and were now into entertaining people at the apartment, both friends and family. Some of those women were simply gorgeous, they loved my mom, were clean-living people, and babysat my sister and I from time to time. One of the women was named Odessa. She was this beautiful redbone woman with freckles, and in later years, so was my first real girlfriend and sexual partner (I have happily not completely recovered from that girlfriend's sensual beauty and our fun dangerous trysts). Odessa appeared single, and I believe she hung around because she was in love with my dad's youngest brother. My mom never appeared jealous of any of the other women. I loved it when my parents would throw parties. Mom would make great finger sandwiches, cut into different shapes with different types of meat or fillings. There would always be leftovers, and my sister and I peeked from our respective bedrooms; the minute my parents exited the apartment to walk their friends to the elevator, we raided the leftovers and ran back to our rooms. My sister and I would also sneak and sip the Manischevitz wine [*we win scheme "it" found we school I in already made*], my parents would always keep a bottle hidden, in the designer glass-topped cabinet coffee table in the living room. It was around this time too that my dad joined the Masons and my mom the Eastern Stars. They were involved attending those meetings for several years, when they abruptly stopped because some mysterious event violently angered my dad. Albeit he remained a loyal Mason his entire life. How do I know?! I could not get him to tell me a single thing about their secrets. I seem to think that caused a slight emotional detachment or breach between he and I. In the end, I should not have cared less. My dad and I became good friends in the waning years, and I have my own secrets to reveal or not reveal!

As I grew up, there were all sorts of things to get into with my little buddies. Snowball fights, rock throwing fights, rubber bands used to shoot paper clips fights, riding on top of elevators, dirt bomb fights, having marble games and competitions with and trading in rare marbles, playing Skellies, and having stairwell races from say the twelfth floor to the first floor—there were two sets of stairwells from each floor—to see who could get to the ground floor first. Typically, I was the best at those kinds of competitions. For example, I was so good at fashioning a snowball for accuracy, I once hit a police officer in the face with a snowball angled from about forty yards away through a half-cracked window in his car. I did not think that I would actually hit him, but I did. I just wanted to see how close I could get. He and his partner stopped, got out of their car, and called me over—none of my buddies were with me that day. I walked over and apologized. The officer was probably pissed, but he was nice to me and faked that I had broken the law and he could take me to jail. Instead, he wrote my name down on a card—what I now suspect was an index card—and told me that I now had *a police record*. He said that from then on, the police would be watching me, and if I did anything wrong *at all*, they would come get me and lock me up. I was young enough at the time to mostly/sort of believe him. I did not truly learn my lesson from that incident, however. At some point when I was a bit older, I was walking inside the park across the street from P.S. 287, between the Fort Greene and Farragut housing projects, when I decided to throw a snowball from the park at a truck driving on Flushing Avenue with his window down. Let me just say, I was on the mark again; and to this day, I am convinced that had I not been the very fast runner with endurance that I was in those days, the driver of that truck would have killed me. He was so angry that he chased me around that park for nothing less than a half hour before giving up and driving off. I had to dive into a large snowbank and hide face first in the cold snow to get away from him.

Although my dad would beat me violently for this or that infraction of his rules or modes of my conduct (like getting caught carving the letters of my first name in my arm, breaking the glass in the designer glass coffee table while horse playing in the living room, and breaking a neighbor's car front windshield during a rock fight. I remember breaking that window vividly as if it happened yesterday. I watched the rock angle toward the windshield and saw it shatter the glass after the rock slipped my grip. I denied I did it. It cost my dad $90 to fund its repair. On our vacation south a week or two later, my dad refused me an extra sandwich because the windshield cost took away from our vacation money.) Once he beat me, after arriving home, for having blurted out, "Look, Mom, there's a man peeing in the street." For some reason, he was totally outraged. I knew that he did not like to hear people curse, but had I cursed?! I was probably all of five or six years old at the time. I felt that I was wronged by that, and I stopped trusting his judgment somewhat after that moment.

Nevertheless, my dad was very supportive of projects that I would involve myself with like: building plastic models of ships, cars, and an aircraft carrier (by the way, the USS # 60 was an aircraft carrier and one of the ships built from scratch during the ten years that we lived on Sand Street), building airplanes out of balsa wood and glue and buying motors and flying them in the grassy area between the buildings [*sing build we thoughts into wee-wee ways . . . bet women area "ass" our "game" . . . we hint*], helping me get supplies for building scooters with wooden crates, two-by-fours and metal skating wheels, buying me an erector set, and a Lionel electric train set. (As an adult, he did not want to return the train set he was keeping for me, claiming that he had bought it for himself. By that time, my nephew had already absconded with the best cars in the set anyway.) When I was around ten or eleven, he helped me build the perfect shoe-shining box and supplied it for me. That is when I started making big money shining shoes across the street outside the main entrance of the Navy Yard. My parents would let me buy pets then. Over time, I had goldfish, a green turtle, and a hamster.

I was probably in the fifth or sixth grade by the time my hamster entered the scene. I really loved that hamster, and I would close my room door, take him out of his cage, and let him wander freely around my room. The only reason I would return him to his cage within a short period of time is that I knew he wanted to exercise on his wheel. I cannot recall whether I purchased my hamster at the pet store, or he was given to me by a Puerto Rican friend that I had at the time. My Puerto Rican friend had always been with me on my jaunts, and he acted like my bodyguard. He would not let anyone get close to me aggressively, so much so that I would often have to call him off. Mind you, by that age, I was a fierce and skilled fisticuffs fighter myself. A lot had transpired between the second grade and then, and I will fill you in on some of those things later. In the interim, I need to tell you about the incident—with a hamster—that ended our friendship. My Puerto Rican buddy spoke broken English, and the only Spanish he wanted to teach me were curse words, and I learned to speak them well. He was constantly saying to me—in the interrogative—what sounded like, "Chew my friend mane?" I would reply, "Of course I'm your friend." However, one uneventful day, after several years of hanging out with him and my other buddies, he asked me to meet him at his apartment, he wanted to show me something. His apartment was located directly below mine and three flights down on the ninth floor, so we shared a similar bedroom panorama. When I arrived at his apartment, we went directly into his bedroom—with his three or four hamsters—and he said, "Watch this." He then calmly picked up one of his hamsters and hurled it out of his ninth-floor window. I do not recall what our immediate verbal exchange was at that moment, but I know that I was on guard. My thoughts were, "This nigga's crazy, let me get out of here before he tries to toss me out the window." After that day, it was somewhat tense for a while between he and I, because I never would have anything to do with him again. But we never physically fought about it.

Years before the hamster incident occurred, I experienced a trauma that changed the trajectory [read to try see joke / women to see we jobs all our times] of my physio-psychological health into my late twenties. I believe I was in the third grade as opposed to the second grade when this was done to me. It was during the elementary school years when a student would have the same teacher for the whole day. For some reason on this day, I had to do #1—urinate—repeatedly, so I had to leave the classroom often and the teacher started loudly complaining to me about having to grant me permission to leave. You know how it goes; I started needing to go so other students started wanting to go as well. At some point not too long before school would be out for the day, I needed to go to do #2—have a bowel movement—and the teacher not only refused to grant me permission to go, but she also made me stand in a corner facing the wall until class ended for the day. Consequently, I defecated on myself. The teacher ended class and left the classroom before the students without looking toward me or saying another word to me. All students knew where to go to exit because as per classroom we had standardized exits from which to leave the building. I managed to slowly get to my exit where, as was routine, I was met by my babysitter, Lois. I told her what happened, and although as we walked the long single block to my building, feces would fall out my pant leg, still forever being the most wonderful babysitter anyone could ever have, she treated me like it was no big deal. She took me home, cleaned me and my clothing up thoroughly, and made me a great snack. Afterward, we were right back into our typical routine. I do not know whether my parents or Lois made an issue of the incident with the teacher or school, but I know that I was never refused access to the restroom again. No matter, I lived with a nervous stomach condition after that for many years. It manifested itself in the following way: whenever I was in groups of people for extended periods or even knew I would be in a group of people for an extended period; the second I could feel the urge to have a bowel movement, my bowels would literally lock up on me as if I were constipated. In fact, I would become constipated immediately and all I could do was give off little silent farts until I was back in a more relaxed circumstance. And every time I would overhear people use the expression "poot-butt" (which was simply a popular expression in those days), no matter what the context, I would feel like they were referring to me. When I would feel in crisis, even if I went and sat on a toilet for a time, nothing would move. What made the situation for me even worse or at least did not help my crisis is the church that my family eventually started attending. I was forced to attend every Sunday and sometimes during the week. It was a storefront church on Fulton Street between Franklin Avenue and Classen. It had a center aisle separating a row of pews on either side all facing the pulpit. The door to the only toilet was adjacent to the pulpit, for all to see. So everyone in the pews would literally *have to* watch you go to and from the toilet during a service. Based on how much time one spent in the toilet everyone would know exactly which function was performed. I cannot express how incredibly insensitive and humiliating I felt that situation to be. At the end, the solution was my consciously releasing the subconscious shame that I felt regarding normal human _evacuation_ [inside out it already you face]. That is, the subconscious shame that I felt when having to take a _shit_ [tell I have sense/ times I shush], when I knew others around me would know that that is what I would be doing. Bottom line(pun), there is no shame in having to take a shit! It is a regular normal human activity. The only issue in your mind should be making sure the toilet seat you use is clean. As to the concern for others: Stop urinating on or leaving your feces on toilet seats in public restrooms! (During my first year in college, my dormitory roommate majored in architecture, and by the end of the year, he was the number one student in his freshmen class. I remember him stating that the most important decision that an architect can make when designing a structure is where to place the restrooms. Because of my earlier experiences in that store front church, I will never forget his *comment*. I feel like I know what torture is!)

There were many things that influenced me and *"impacted"* me (do not miss the pun) between the time of the incident in the third grade and my graduation from sixth grade. There were the major family picnics, where family elements from both sides of the East River would meet at various beaches and upstate New York and New Jersey daytime camping areas to eat and frolic. There were trips to Hudson, New York, where my mom's youngest sister and husband owned a fun bar and grill. As I transitioned from my babysitter Lois to my aunt Kevie, I started spending a lot of time in the Fort Greene (FG) projects at my aunt's house and making a separate set of friends there. In addition to my aunt Kevie being the best pastry and cakemaker in the family (her layered coconut pineapple cake could make you "slap your momma"), my teenaged male cousin taught me how to make zip-guns (the barrels of which were cut from stolen metal auto antennas, one rung of which could perfectly fit a 22 long rifle bullet), took me to hang out with his Fort Greene Chaplains gang buddies, and I and my new young friends there discovered the wonders of the <u>Library</u> [*women are bar I live/evil women are bra I like*]. Also listening to and watching Little Anthony and the Imperials *rehearsing* [*sing are* already here] in the stairwells of the projects before they became famous was a special treat for me.

One book that my few young Fort Greene friends and I discovered in the library opened my eyes to the concept of *thought,* as a separate *thing in itself,* and later in life, viewing thought as a *thing inside itself* and *of itself.* The library was located adjacent to the FG projects and across the street from Cumberland hospital. Cumberland hospital is where in the third grade—under *ether*—I had an appendectomy performed. (Now that I am reminded of when I had my appendix removed, I know that it was my second-grade teacher who made me stand face first in a corner of our classroom until I was forced to defecate on myself.

18

Yep, I guess I still feel some kind of way about that _bitch_ [_head sees I bad times / choice it be_].) The book that we discovered in the library was a _medical anatomy book_ [book women meant to anal area _I med_], initially housed in the stacks and not in a reference section. We would be very discreet or secretive when looking through it because we clearly understood it was for adult viewing. It contained colorized photos of adult male and female organs in various forms of health and disease. For example, a penis ravaged by syphilis. It had photos of childbirth and a sequenced and colorized assembly of the organs of the body on Cellophane-type pages. The day after the librarian caught us looking through the book, it was placed out of our reach in the reference section behind her desk. No matter, what the book alerted me to was all of the information potentially hidden in library books in general. So I got my mom to help me get a library card and I became an avid reader, more like a bibliophile, a bookworm. The anatomy book initially piqued my interest in gynecology. I rationalized that idea quickly. The archetype had already been set in my psyche. My immediate thoughts were that after following through with all the hard work it would take to become a doctor, my practice would likely not flourish. What white women or light-skinned Black women would want this dark-skinned Black man viewing much less fidgeting around with their vaginas.

Understanding the existing politics and social structure of the time, I concluded that I would be ridiculed and simply viewed as a pervert, as the reasoning behind my having an interest in that type of medicine. So I abandoned any additional interest in my initial career goal and settled in on just reading a variety of books, looking up words, and developing and improving my penmanship. I read Aesop's fables, Grimm's stories, Edgar Allen Poe's works, Robert Frost poems, the Time-Life series of books, etc. My parents bought me a five or six inched thick single volume encyclopedia; that was my go-to book for basic information on any topic. That book served as my work horse through the ninth grade. I still preserve that book and my Time-Life

19

series book on _mathematics_ [_senses see I after them . . . already made / senses I see after me thoughts "aftermath"_] to this day.

Meanwhile, back at my own area in the Farragut projects, I had my new best buddy to hang out with, James R. He lived in Betty T's building and we both knew how cute she was, so in our minds we were in competition to win her favor and/or affection. I did not push the issue between James, Betty, and I because I had empathy for him. First, there were more pretty girls in my building than there were in his. Second, his dad would not just beat him violently for offenses. His dad was _absolutely_ [_women love we times you lick sins obviously best area_] merciless toward him and I rarely would see his mom. The first time I witnessed his dad beat him, he beat him in his head with a broom handle. The second time I saw his dad beat him was the last time I would enter his apartment; in fact, I may not have been allowed in his apartment after that incident. That time his dad beat James senselessly, and with an ironing cord. I would never have entered his apartment again anyway; because after what I had witnessed that day, I had to shy away and divorce my mind from the idea of killing his dad, which I had the means to do. Not too long after that incident with James, I warned my own dad about ever putting his hands on me again. I was in my early teens, and with that _stance_ [we see end all stop], the episodes were ended.

Back on my side of the street, I had exotic marbles to win, the twin Michell brothers to routinely coax outside and beat up, scooters to build and ride, Marines to watch in their dress blues and holstered 45's change their guards. (Once while I was watching the Marines change guards, the automatic pistol went off and a bullet went into the ceiling. They did not miss a stroke. They stood at attention as a higher-ranking officer came out of the office, emptied and exchanged the weapon that had been fired. The fresh guard then chambered and holstered the new weapon and the three _saluted_ [_during me time you_ *loved area sin*] ending the exchange.) Part of our fun activities in those days was to sneak into the Yard and bait the Marines, so that they could chase us out through the main gate. We would have piles of rocks already set up. And as the Marines came chasing us through the gate, we would suddenly stop, turn, and start hurling rocks at them. Those tough guys loved it! Another thing that they would do is let us guys watch as they would bend, put their foreheads to the end of a baseball bat, run around in a circle for a few times, and then try to run straight. They loved that game too and it was the funniest thing to watch. Still there were girls in the building to steal a kiss on the cheek and run from. The girls pretended to hate it, but in truth they loved it. It made them feel special, because aside from always standing and talking in the spot where we could sneak up on them, and the little love tap they would give us when we returned to the scene; we were all the best of friends. However, one time I kissed Yvonne C. on the cheek, ran, and tripped jumping over a low-lying chain-linked fence. I fell hitting and scraping the skin—to the white—off one side of my face. That was the end of the steal a kiss and run game for me. I went upstairs bloodied, and it took months of cocoa butter applications for my skin's flesh tone to return.

At some point, shining shoes at the main entrance of the Yard became my thing to do immediately after school and on the weekends. I made the money to buy my Converse high-top sneakers, airplane parts, candy and snacks, accessories for my bikes, and clothes. My parents had purchased me a beautiful blood-red 10-speed bike with white-walled tires one Christmas, that my mother's brother Marion taught me to ride. I bought brakes and generators to power the lights and siren I put on the bike. I bought an air pump for tires, tire patches, glue, kick stand, special handlebars, and replacement spokes. My bike became my car, and I knew everything about repairing bikes. In fact, I started building fixed wheel bikes. I would remove the 10-speed gear and replace the rear wheel sprocket with a 9-tooth sprocket. The power to move the bike came directly from your legs. They were fast bikes, and you could not stop them suddenly without special breaks or having the space and time to slow them down by skidding the tires from quickly lifting the rear wheel and backpedaling. I was the designated bike repairman, albeit I would teach my buddies what I knew. The lower Brooklyn Bridge area became wide open to us. There was "dead man's hill" on the other side of the bridge near the Natural Lamb skin prophylactic factory. There was also the trophy factory, the Swiss ice cream factory, the Dutch Boy paint factory [women our open fact aint poor. Women often "butch" denies we thoughts.]. I believe the Busta Brown Shoes factory [why or fact some hoes own bar-street-you be we thoughts] was there along with still other factories and the docks to explore and hang out around.

For some reason, perhaps my gift of gab, I was often the leader of the group depending on what set of guys were in the pack at a given moment. In either case, my opinion always mattered. One day when I was the lead man, and we were fooling around dangerously on some dilapidated docks, a couple or three white men in suits, hats, and overcoats approached me. The one guy was friendly and asked if I could get my other buddies to listen to me and agree with what I would instruct them to do. I told him yes. We are a team. He then handed me some paper money to take and share with my buddies and asked that we stop playing on the docks, because he was the owner, and the docks were too dangerous for us to be walking around on. I promised him that we would *not* play there again, and we did not. I did not know who he was then, but some years later, I saw his picture in the *Daily News*. He had been shot and killed at a lower Manhattan barbershop in broad daylight. His name was Albert Anastasia, the Italian gangster leader of Murder Inc.

During those years, I had grown from a toddler in nursery school, to being babysat, to being a "latchkey," kid bringing myself home from school, carefully unlocking and locking the door behind me, and not opening the door for "anyone" until my mom or dad got home, to roaming in all areas of downtown Brooklyn. (Once my mom recounted an incident where when I was once home alone, and a family friend came to the door to return something. I told him that if it could fit under the door, he could return it. If not, he was plainly out of luck.) In my youth, I was generally aware that Italians lived in neighborhoods all around us, and that there was a strong Mafia presence there like the Gallo brothers; but it appeared that we all lived in relative harmony. In my immediate consciousness was the _Fort Greene Chaplains_ [_sin already licks pubic area . . . hair see we enter wee-wee . . . hour got time, for_] and the _Farragut_ [_time you got out already . . . our area is fine_] projects _Puerto Rican_ [_can I hour opening touch pure?!_] street gang the _Sand Street Angels_ [_same angle times wee-wee are straight and seen_]. My first cousin was the War Lord of the FG Chaplains and I knew the Cape Man (always wore a cape) and the Umbrella Man (always wore a hat and carried an umbrella), the two leaders of the Sand Street Angels. There was another mysterious gang called the Baldies [sin we idea . . . licks _area bad_]. I never saw or met any of them. However, when word circulated around the two projects that the "Baldies were coming" on a given night, both youth and adults would remain inside. You would see no movement on the streets in our neighborhood. The chaplains had chapters all over Brooklyn, and their primary rivals were called the bishops. The Sand Street Angels was a small gang with perhaps thirty members, but they were touted to have broken into a national guard army and stolen a cache of weapons making them a formidable opponent. I believe that they eventually morphed into the Young Lords / Vice Lords, but I could be mistaken. In the interim, the Angels would be seen roaming Farragut all the time, until my sister's boyfriend from FG was stabbed to death on the Flushing Avenue side of P.S. 287, as he was returning home one early evening from visiting her. No one was sure who actually did it, because he would visit her regularly without incident, and he had never expressed any concerns for his safety. No matter, the chaplains would have been certain to enact harsh retribution on the suspected Angels, so they were nowhere to be found. The next time I heard of the Angels was when the _Cape Man_ [man "we" penis (pen is) already seen] and the _Umbrella Man_ [man already well be . . . mind you] turned up being sought for the broad daylight fatal stabbing of a few white males in a park in the _Hell's Kitchen_ [enter we itch . . . kept . . . scene hell] area of Manhattan. Months later, they were captured eating from garbage cans in Manhattan. Their circumstances upon arrest stood out in my mind because they were both good looking and they were always—and I do mean always—well dressed.

In the warmer months, my sister and I "stayed" doing things outdoors. In the colder months, my sister would be visiting her numerous girlfriends and I would be getting into mischief with my buddies in the hallways, lobby, vestibule, and stairwells of the building, when away from my apartment, because I loved being alone in my room reading, playing with my pets and toys like my "erector" set, and looking out my window across the river and also into the shipyard observing shipping-lane activity. It was in the stairwells that we once feasted—to the point of being beyond sated, bloated—on the spoils of an unlocked pastry truck (I want to say Drake's pastries) its driver was forced to abandon, which was intractably stuck in feet's deep snow in the roadway behind our building. To our mischievous _good fortune_ and _keen observation,_ the driver walked away having forgotten to lock the truck's delivery door. At other times, we would sit on the steps of the stairwell and discuss important matters like how to rig an abandoned TV picture tube (they were huge and thick in those days) so that we could attach it to a long jump rope rapped over the ceiling water-pipe bars in the basement, releasing it to cause what sounded like a bomb going off in the basement. Once we took a ruler and sat and measured our penises, and we had an extended discussion about how long it would be before we would all grow a lot of pubic hair, and whether there was anything that we could apply to our bodies to speed up the process. One brilliantly idiotic suggestion was regularly rubbing onion juice in one's pubic area.

Speaking of pubic hair, I recall—while in undergraduate school— living off campus in the rear apartment of a house fashioned into a duplex and adjacent to a small apartment complex and directly in front of a two-story four-family apartment building sealed off from Ashe Street by my apartment; and being introduced to a reclusive neighbor, most others being very friendly, sociable, and gregarious. We other residents were all coupled off and would often sleep overnight as couples around a small kidney-shaped pool, where we would toss in 100-pound blocks of ice to cool down the water temperature, when we were enduring summer times when it could easily be 110 degrees or more at eleven o'clock at night. We did not have to deal with mosquitos in Arizona, so it was great fun. The loner would typically only allow my friend Bob O. to enter his apartment separated from the others near the pool. At any rate, Bob convinced him to let me enter one day. His apartment was very clean and well-organized with stacks of a variety of pornographic types of materials—books, magazines, and films. Bob took me there because he wanted me to see this one book. It was a medical book about 12 x 14 x 3 inches in dimensions, and it was filled with color photos, with minimal written text, of the pubic hair area of hundreds if not several thousands of predominately individual white women. What the book made abundantly clear was just how unique the pubic hair area patterns are for each individual woman. It was like one's individual fingerprint. And in that instant, just like the library anatomy book had done, my view of the world was _critically impacted_ [Do cite a page mean women live life already sees I see wit / Do we impact ally critic/education act power I am ally critic.].

Looking back, that _mensurable_ [_able are us men_] act that my "boys" and I did in the stairwells was an _inflexion point_ [_talk in open on pussy . . . I sex we like found . . . entered I_] for us. I had always been focused on fighting skills—even reading *ring magazine* [*we into I scheme already gained areas mind . . . ring*]—until that time, because I was always one of the shortest in the groups and floated around from building to building in the projects, people would *test* me. And I could fight! Somewhere along the way, I thought that when in a fight if I hit harder than the other guy, I had the advantage. And it worked, I became tough like my *Uncle George* [*we game ours open we ground entry clue*], win at any cost. At one point, I got into a fight in the playground at the rear of my building, and a white priest in a priest's habit came and broke it up. He offered us the opportunity to finish the fight inside the community center located in the basement of the building next to mine. He made us put on these large sixteen (16) ounce gloves and discussed us joining the *Police Athletic League (PAL)* [*we you got already . . . we licked . . . see I times we liked head after we see I loved offering person*]. I loved the concept of competing against others in boxing, but after continuing our fight with gloves on, I trashed the idea. I could not see well enough with those big gloves on, and I was not used to getting hit in the face. Every time I would throw a punch and withdraw my glove, when I peeked out to throw another punch I would too frequently get hit in the face. I did not get seriously hurt, but I was completely frustrated. I could not tell if I had won the fight or not. No matter, I usually later became friends with the guys I fought anyway. But yes, I concluded that I would rather just use my bare fists to fight. I could do more delivering than receiving punches in that way.

Meanwhile, back in the stairwells, our conversations were now switching from being tough guys to impressing the girls we liked, dressing well, and *also doing well in school.* (I always did dress well because my parents tailormade a lot of my clothes, like overcoats and suits. My family would make fun trips to Delancey Street, in its heyday, in Manhattan to buy garment materials.) Yet something else was in process during that *proximate* [*eat made I sex pro / mate I sex obviously our purpose*] period in time. Our bodies, male and female, were literally changing. Some of the guys were quickly growing taller and our individual interests, consequently, were changing as well. Bike riding in groups switched over to basketball [*all be times we ask best / live life already . . . bet, ask, be*] for some and Spalding pink handball [live life already . . . *be hand . . . ink pen game. In laid spell*] for others. I became a card-carrying member of the Smokey the Bear [hear, bet, key out mind . . . sin] club and literally joined the Blue Jackets [set kept . . . see already "we" joke . . . you lick butt]; the naval equivalent of the Boy Scouts [sin out . . . see sense . . . women obviously best (be street)!]. We would meet in the gym of my elementary school P.S. 287, wearing beautiful US Navy blue quality uniforms, with award ribbons, authentic navy belts, and spats, etc. We would have "sham" battles with water balloons or paper bags filled with white flour. Once we took a ferry and went to one of the islands in the harbor near New York City and watched a mock amphibious landing and a full military battle with uniformed soldiers and weapons giving off the sounds and smoke of battle. Around that same time, my dad's youngest brother—a merchant marine [*we win already . . . mine chant . . . hour me*]—would take me with him to his ship to pick up things, when he docked at a pier on the Hudson River off Manhattan. This was in the days when the Queen Mary [way men enter wee-wee you question] and *the* Queen Elizabeth [hear bet already . . . lie, scheme . . . enter wee-wee you *quest*] ocean liners were still docking at piers in Manhattan. Most times I would wait for him in his car or go with him to admire those huge ships, while noticing all the feces and condoms that floated in the Hudson River at the time. Once he took me on board his ship and I observed just how luxurious even a cargo ship can be. My uncle was the electrical engineer on his ships.

In the interim, the girls we knew were changing too. Their manner and attitudes were changing. Of course, they were experiencing their menstruation cycles [*sensed we looked . . . sees women see, No. I after you our straight men*] and filling out physically. They started being particular about which guys they wanted to spend not just time with but be alone time with. This arbitrary male female shuffling and the other things I have mentioned caused our larger group to go in different directions most of the time. I started going to Fort Greene to hang out, go play handball, and go to the Majestic movie theater (the Mighty Mo as we called it) to watch Westerns and movies like *Rodan*, *The Blob*, and *King Kong*, and Westerns on the big screen. Food concessions were inexpensive in those days. Three dollars could get you in the movie and have you _sated_ [*did eat some*] before you left. The Mighty Mo was located roughly in that area in downtown Brooklyn where DeKalb Avenue, Fulton Street, and Flatbush Avenue meet in front of the Fox theater in the then major shopping area, downtown Fulton Street, where the major landmarks were Brooklyn Tech H.S., the Fox and Paramount theaters, and Junior's pastry restaurant. The girls had not romantically noticed me yet, and my parents had joined a church pastored by Reverend Jethro J., so we were often away from the area on weekends when everyone else was scouting about in the projects. However, I still liked Betty T. and she, James R. and I were in the same class in the fifth grade. We were in class 5-1 together, which meant we were the highest achieving students who entered fifth grade at our school. Our teacher was _Mrs. Zimmerman_ [*man are we mad . . . meant . . . I screamed since we mind*]. I sat behind both Betty and James. One day I decided to play a prank on James with Betty. I had him unwittingly pass a note I had written to Betty. The note read: Betty I want some pussy . . . James! Had I had any common sense, I would not have written the note, because Betty immediately handed the note to Mrs. Zimmerman. Mrs. Zimmerman read the note, gave the class an assignment, left the room, and spoke to the teacher in the class across the hall. When she returned along with the other teacher, she left the classroom door open and informed the class that the teacher would be monitoring our classroom while she attended to something, which was not uncommon. She then left the room again and I sensed that something major was afoot. When she returned the second time, she walked directly over to me and told me to grab my things. She must have taken me around to every teacher on that floor and said, "This is him." In the end, she took me to the "remedial" class 5-5 and told me that I was officially in that class from then on. It must have taken me days to figure out how she knew it was me who wrote the note and so fast?! (The answer was revealed when a soft voice must have whispered to me and said, "Try considering that the note was written in your own handwriting . . . dummy!")

The teacher in the new class was male and I regret that I do not recall his name. As it turned out, it was one of the best things that ever happened to me. There were fewer students in the new classroom, and he was a great teacher and a great person. In the previous classroom, I would play around a lot and not really focus on learning. In the new section, I took learning more seriously and we did nonstandard things, like learning to play chess—I recall that I placed in several intermural chess competitions—and mastering arithmetic. (Arithmetic is what most people are referring to when they say they hate math. And believe it or not, it is the failure to master arithmetic properly that has failed many a calculus student, for example, not understanding how to divide fractions—a.k.a. rational expressions in calculus. Mathematics as mathematics does not truly begin until calculus.) I also was entered into a New York City science fair and received honorable mention behind the winner who designed a mini volcano. My project sprang from me feeling some kind of way about bank robberies. I recall watching the infamous bank robber <u>Willie Sutton</u> [no/know time told us lie like I would] being interviewed upon his capture. He was asked why he robbed so many banks and he replied, "Because that's where the money's at!" So I thought about all the Western bank robbery movies I had enjoyed watching; <u>John Dillinger</u> [linger like I do . . . enter/ end head opens joy] batteries and designed a mock-up of a bank with teller windows, etc. At the entrance, the potential robber would have to enter through two sets of doors with bulletproof glass. In the floor of what effectively would be a box formed by the sets of doors would be placed sensors. As the robber would go to leave the bank, the teller activated sensors in the floor would automatically lock the inner door and the robber's bodyweight would lock the outer door, trapping the robber and automatically signaling the nearest police station. I do not know how many times over the years that I have seen kids exhibiting their volcano design in commercials and movies as *original* science projects. I have also seen my concept used in several movies; and more *poignantly* [*women* love time in area . . . enter game I output], every time I stop at a modern working stoplight that has had an inordinate delay, and I inch my car up to shift its weight on the roadway and the light then *immediately* [women lacking eat idea . . . we *mean . . . I mind*] changes—due to the sensors in the roadway—I am reminded of my concept. At any rate, my school also honored me on the assembly stage with a certificate like what the science fair officials gave me. By the sixth grade, I was back on my game academically and was appointed a student crossing guard, with a metal badge shaped like a police badge and the wide white fake-leather plastic belt that strapped diagonally across my chest and buckled around my waist. I rarely buckled the belt because that did not look cool enough. And trust me, all the other students in the school thought I was "the shit."

I was in the sixth or seventh grade when I first experienced consensual sex. It happened several times that year and over a few subsequent years with the same two girls. And they taught me! In the first instance she was a beautiful redbone girl with reddish brown hair and freckles. I had been walking in the projects with several of my boys when I first noticed her and commented. My friend Allen B—who lived on my floor, had grown taller than me, and whose dad they called Judge—replied that I should not even try to get to know her; being that he had tried several times and had been rebuffed. Another one of the guys walking with us concurred. I replied, "Just because she is not interested in either of you does not mean she would not be interested in me." At some point, I approached her and within two weeks we were an item. (What is ironic is that the first time I met Allen B's dad and we spoke, I had said to him:

"They call you Judge, but I bet that you cannot judge me.") She was *articulate* [*eat like you see I art* / late you see it . . . ours *already* {women read looks always}], intelligent, sexy, warm, gentle, and fearless. We would secret ourselves in some challenging public and not-so-public places, and she always wore dresses for easy access. What really had me smitten with her was her shape, skin tone, soft, thick hair, and hairy bush. She was an inflection point in my life, because I have never *recovered* [down we often see we are / did we cover we are] from her affection. Since then, I have always been my most turned on by women who are very hairy in that area, unlike a lot of these punk males who think that female body hair is nasty or unclean, while failing to appreciate pubic hair patterns are unique to each woman and accentuates her beauty. Moreover, pubic hair helps to thwart STDs.

The other girl that I initially got involved with that year I met at church. She was one of Reverend Jethro's children. She was cute, sensuous, with a different skin tone, and had a beautiful hourglass shape. She just really had the "hots" for me, and it turned me on, so we made it happen. The first time was at my family's apartment on Sand Street. Since both our families were very close, we created some ruse—I believe using my sister as the ploy—for her having to stay at our apartment for several hours, before we returned to church for a Sunday evening service. And we almost got caught by my mother! I set up shop in the bathroom, after Sunday dinner and upon my parents having settled down to relax and catnap in the living room, my sister was staying out of the way in her bedroom. She knew that we liked each other and wanted to be left alone together. I filled the bathtub with water and brought my battery-powered motorboat and my cereal box acquired toy submarine pretending to be simply playing with those toys in the tub. I left the door open to help avoid any suspicion and listen for my parents. We got busy, and at some point, I could hear my mom coming. I had an erection and had no time to put my penis in my pants, so I dropped to my knees and leaned with my pecker [*are we kept . . . see we play?!]* out and pressed against the cold tub fiddling with my toys; and with my back to my mom as she and I spoke about what I was doing. She appeared satisfied with my explanation of my activities, went and checked on my sister, and then she returned to the living room. We minimized our sensual activities after that encounter and whispered plans for potentially more secure and private ways of getting together, which we did from time to time.

Speaking of "pecker," I am reminded of a large beautifully multicolored <u>woodpecker</u> [*are we kept . . . see we play do woo*] that built a nest in a tree directly outside my apartment on Ashe Street in Tempe, Arizona. My tuxedo appointed black-and-white patched cat, Country, sat on a windowsill hour after hour, intensely watching the action, over the days it took for the woodpecker to finish its nest. My cat, Country, was a bonified hunter and fighter. Normally he would refuse to be kept in the house after dark. I would often hear him outside fighting, and I had to break him from killing doves and dropping them at my door in the mornings. Once he dropped a bat at the door that was wounded but not dead, it could not fly but lay grinding its teeth. I put it in a jar, had it tested, and fortunately, it was not rabid. At any rate, once the woodpecker had finished its nest, I could not keep my cat in the house during the daytime. And I was entertained, as Country spent many days frustrating himself trying to reach the woodpecker's hole, that had been cleverly notched just out of his reach. There were no branches on the tree below the opening to the nest, and if ever Country's paw would nearly reach the very top edge of the hole, he would be just enough off balance to fall to the ground and which he rarely allowed himself to do.

I remember the seventh grade being a challenge. I had multiple fights, in school and after school, having had to switch from elementary school to a junior high school (Sands JHS 265) located some distance from my immediate neighborhood and encountering new unfamiliar faces and personalities. The kids my age in the school got to know me from my fists, how well I dressed, and my intellect. However, there were a couple of non-student older teenagers that I had to constantly keep finding ways to avoid, because they kept coming around strong-arming lunch money from my fellow seventh-grade students in the school yard, before the start of school in the morning. They had burned me once when they first started coming around. I would most often not carry a bag lunch to school, because I always had money made from my job shining sailor's shoes at the Navy Yard, and I had to walk a long way to get to school. Each day I would bring enough money to buy my typical lunch at the corner deli immediately across the street from our school. My lunch would consist of a quart soda, a raisin-cinnamon roll, and a foot-long "hero sandwich." I would eat half the sandwich, the cinnamon roll, and save the other half for a snack when I got home. (Modern-day subway sandwiches do not come close to having the quality and taste of those deli sandwiches.) So I had to protect my lunch money. I knew that the two guys were not chaplains, because I had never seen them before. Yet I could no longer seek protection from my warlord cousin, because the court had plea bargained his removal from New York State; his de facto involvement in the day-long gang battle that took place at Coney Island in the late 1950s and his gang's shooting up the "penny arcade" [read see a New York pen] on Flatbush Avenue across from Junior's restaurant. (That is when I learned that my cousin was not the worst of the street gang warlords in Brooklyn. He was apparently levelheaded as compared to some and tried to negotiate out of potentially major bloodshed situations. For example, he did not allow guns to be used at the Coney Island battle. How I know is because he took me with him to retrieve and carry the gun[s] used in shooting up of the Penny arcade. When we returned to the "paradise" [the outdoor hangout], I was privy to the gang leader's discussion about the instructions my cousin had given for that particular shooting and other events that he had planned out.) However, I do know that after the Italians allegedly killed one of the non-gang member innocents under a section of the

Brooklyn Queens Expressway across from the projects; by cutting his throat with a machete and hanging him upside-down, they started finding a lot of bodies other than chaplains in Fort Greene Park. (My parents and I drove by the bloody scene, when returning from a church service the night it happened.) The guy they killed that night was, like my sister's boyfriend, very nice and a non-gang member. Again, as for my cousin, _Corny_ [women into hours obviously see], he had to move to _Florida_ [indict I for leave] and live with my mom's oldest sister until he reached over twenty-one.

One day two detectives came to my homeroom class and asked whether anyone could identify the two older teens who were stealing money from the kids in the school yard. All the students in the room knew who they were, but I was the only one that acknowledged I could. They asked if I did identify them would I be willing to testify against them in court and I said yes. They then took me to a police lineup, and I picked the two of them out. I was then immediately returned to school. Some days or weeks later, the detectives arranged to pull me from class again, and I went to a courtroom where I testified under oath to their actions. After my testimony, I had to wait in the hallway outside the courtroom for some time. When I was returned to the courtroom, the judge praised me for having the courage to come forth and testify. Then, having found them guilty of some charges, he sentenced them to juvenile hall. They were never seen at our school again.

The eighth grade represents a very formative period in my life. During my summer family two-week vacation, my two closest active best friends at the time had been introduced to and joined Reverend Arturo Skinner's large young people's church on DeKalb Avenue. What was so stunning about that was first of all, I was the one going to church every Sunday with my by then deacon dad and family. They both came from single-parent female households, and they were my more academically achieved and best behavior inclined influential elements, among my larger group of buddies. They had started me on the way to not getting into so many fights. They had literally become serious born-again Christians overnight. The most that I could testify to at that time was having been awarded my very own King James Version of the scriptures for having had perfect attendance in Sunday school for three consecutive months at my church and having received a water baptism at eight years old. Both Joseph T. and Sumner L. were very good-looking light-skinned young men. Joseph T. was our fastest neighborhood track star and Sumner L. brought home the best report cards and was involved in school politics. Each of us thought highly of one another. I visited their church soon afterward and could rightly understand the immediate draw. The church was large and full of some of the most beautiful young Black people in Brooklyn. And when their young people's mass choir jumped on the song "We've come this far by faith," I could literally feel the spirit of God. While back in my own church, I was one of the lead singers in the junior choir—with the congregation favoring my leading the song "Only Believe," and a Sunday <u>school lesson</u> [*no less cool head sense*] leader.

When we returned to school after the summer break and upon entering the eighth grade, I remember that the three of us picked up a fourth really close friend. Our hangout group became Joseph T., Sumner L., Jeffrey C., and I, Larry J. As it happened, Jeffrey C. joined Joseph T. in being the second fastest on the track team. (I no longer could run due to a foot injury sustained during a multi-family beach outing, where I ripped open my right foot on a piece of broken glass, into the bone at the base of my right pinky toe. It probably would have healed properly, had not my "fire-waving, roach-fighting aunt" walked up behind everyone and ***thrown salt into the wound*** [wound he thinks to enter I talk . . . life already senses . . . own our thoughts], as I lay on my back and other family members were removing fragments of glass from my foot. I will not try to describe the secondary pain resulting from that application of salt.) At school, it seems like the four of us were always together. We called ourselves the _Chessmen_ [men . . . same sense we heads see]. As the Chessmen, we made plans to pool our monies and rent a house as a clubhouse, but we never settled on the idea, because, after locating a potential house, we got bogged down over whether spending money on the look of the exterior of the house was more important than making the interior of the house fabulous. At some point, Joseph and Jeffrey would participate in, and Sumner and I would attend, track meets at the 168th Street armory in _Manhattan_ [_entering before-after heals man_]. You should have seen all of those beautiful Black girls drooling over the runners. And you should have felt the pride that I felt watching my fellow young Black people exhibiting such grace, beauty, and class, on and off the track.

Academically, my eighth grade revolved around my English class. During that one year, we read books like _Of Human Bondage, Crime and Punishment_, some of _The Iliad and the Odyssey_, The Good Earth [_thoughts dear hoe got_], The Grapes of Wrath [_thoughts raw . . . find out rapes get hands_], The Tropic of Cancer [_hours we see can find out her times topic_] (a book which my teacher had us cover in brown shopping bag paper in order to conceal it in school), some Shakespeare [_we are all she speak_] and others. I still remember a line in the earliest pages of _The Tropic of Cancer_, where the author writes, "Oh Tania, where is that warm cunt of yours." We also read poetry and short stories and learned the analysis of these written materials. We went on outings to operas like _Fiorello, Rigoletto, Westside Story_, and The Barber of Seville [_see fill . . . found out ours be bar we thoughts_]. And I gave no thought to the idea that the authors were white, and they might be miseducating me, because at that level and quality of learning, it is not even relevant, even today. I was only concerned with the content of the stories, the word definitions and the styles of expression, they were art forms. It was a lot of hard work, but the learning was so fun and fulfilling that I did not feel the pain. And I only recall two fights in the eighth grade. One was in my English class with a clown I had bounced around the previous year, in my shop class, for doing the exact same thing, hiding my books and/or my personal belongings when I had to leave the room for something. I started punching that anus so fiercely in my English class that my teacher threw a chair in my direction to get me to stop. I told the story to my third-grade babysitter, and she got upset over the teacher having done that. As for me, even at the time, I thought he was cool and had done the right thing. In another situation, I was standing outside on the sidewalk talking with a female friend. I recall that I was wearing a light purple shirt with a black valor vest, and Florsheim loafers knowing I looked cool. This effeminate acting boy came up and entered the conversation. I could tell that he liked the girl I was talking to and that she knew and was friendly with him. So I did not mind him entering the conversation. In fact, I noticed a tie clip that he was wearing and had obviously designed and made in metal shop. I touched the tie clip and simultaneously complimented him on its workmanship. As I turned to continue talking to my female friend, he blindsided me with a punch that almost knocked me out. I saw stars for a few seconds, but I grabbed him and held on for the instant I needed to restore my balance. I then proceeded to start whipping his ass good, but I could not finish because the bell to enter school rang. He ran and I yelled a promise to get back at him after school. When I looked down, I had blood on my shirt. I looked for him all day <u>between</u> [*into wee-wee ways . . . bet*] classes and did not see him. I looked for him after school and saw him running away really fast in the distance. I then saw the girl whom I had been speaking with when it happened. She told me she suggested during classes for him to run home after school. She obviously knew what I was going to do for him. He ran home like that every day for over a week, until I got tired of seeing him run. And I was no longer angry enough to whip his ass like I would have earlier. So I told her to tell him I would no longer seek to hurt him, and the next day to come and make peace with me. We did and the three of us restored friendly ways, but I never trusted him enough to stand too close to him after that.

By the end of my eighth grade, the US Navy had announced that they were closing the Brooklyn naval shipyard. The navy offered my dad a job at the naval shipyard in Newport News, Virginia; but neither of my parents wished to relocate there. So we moved from the Sand Street Farragut housing projects into a three-family brownstone house my parents purchased on Quincy Street—near Bedford Avenue—in the Bedford-Stuyvesant section of Brooklyn, during the summer before entering my ninth grade at Sands Junior High School. Consequently, rather than change junior high schools a year before graduating with my immediate birth cohort, I commuted by city bus to my same school that last year. Commuting to school, trying to actively maintain all of my old friendships, while socially acclimating to a completely new style of neighborhood was an exciting, adventurous, and fun task. It was a relatively easy transition for me, because I was never of that energy where I had to remain around what I had always been around. In other words, I was not afraid to move and make new friends. I was never the lonely type. And by the way, not only had our family home moved, but by then our church home had relocated from Reid Avenue to a location on Fulton Street within walking distance of our house. We lived on Quincy Street between Franklin and Bedford Avenue which runs parallel to Lexington and Gates avenues. Some of the major landmarks in that area were the Bedford YMCA, Boys and Girls High School, the Concord or Cornerstone Baptist (pastored by the eminent orator Gardner C. Taylor), and the Muslim mosque a few blocks up on Bedford Avenue, where after church on Sundays I would go and listen to Malcolm X speak. Our house bordered the rear of the butcher store whose entrance faced Bedford Avenue. The first friend that I made, Eric H., worked as a home delivery person for the butcher store. On that same side of the street was a Chinese laundry, a Black-owned candy store, the best of its kind, and an A and P supermarket. Going in the opposite direction on Bedford and on the same side of the street crossing over Quincy Street was a Black-owned grocery store, that my parents would eventually come to own, Cowboys pool hall, a neighborhood restaurant, and a dry cleaner. The second male friend that I made, Clayton O., was Panamanian and lived with his mother and younger brother over the grocery store. Eric was out of school and Clayton was in his first year at Boys high school, and an honor student. Across the light on Quincy at Bedford, and on my side of the street was the "paradise" or hang out of the chaplains <u>"Comanche" chapter</u> [Our we time? People ahead sees he can. Man overseas/oversees] of the <u>Chaplains</u> [*sin already looks perfect . . . ahead sees*] street gang. Seven days a week, the "Big" people and the "Little" people subgroup of the Comanches would be seen fraternizing in direct view of me and my house. They would stare at me, and I would stare back at them yet we never spoke; even when they walked past me as I stood watching the expert play of pimps and hustlers playing nine ball, for hundreds of dollars per game, at Cowboys pool hall. By the way, <u>Cowboy</u> [*women obviously be way overseas*] was from Sumatra, in Indonesia. The adult leader of the Comanche gave me the impression that he liked my, what C.G. Jung would call, persona, the Sunday-churchgoing and weekday-schoolbook-carrying school kid, so the leader of the little people, Scooter, and his crew never bothered me, until I initiated a conversation with Scooter. Prior to that, to the person, they all seemed like nice humorous and fun-loving guys. Yet we were in proximity so frequently, I felt comfortable that we were familiar with each other enough. So one day while returning from school on a city bus, I spotted Scooter and another of his boys running out of and being chased by the owner of a Chinese laundry two blocks from my house. They had apparently snatched cash from the register. A few minutes later, we were passing each other close to the candy store near my house; and I jokingly, but foolishly, asked Scooter: How much did you get? (I was attempting to use the incident as an opportunity to initiate direct conversation with Scooter, despite not approving of what he had done.) He began yelling at me and we almost came to blows, but rather than fight me, he walked away. No doubt he could tell from my stance and fearless posture that I could probably beat him. Later that evening after dark, I had been sitting in the butcher store talking with my friend, Eric, as I typically would do before the store's closing time. As I left the store, two people grabbed my arms from behind, Scooter jumped in my face loudly mouthing off, and his friend punched me in the face using brass knuckles. Immediately my friend Eric and several adult men jumped into the fray, and we all started fighting. In short order, my help started yelling at me, "Run home," and I did. When I got inside my house, I walked directly into the kitchen, past the door where my parents were seated in the living room, but unconsciously did not turn on the light when I got to the kitchen, being lost in reflection. My mom immediately came into the kitchen asking what was wrong. I said nothing was wrong, but she turned on the lights and could see I was bleeding from the mouth. A few minutes later, many of the gang members, including the adult overall leaders, were at our house banging on the front door and windows demanding I come out. My dad grabbed [*down we be is already our gain / bed be already our game*] his shotgun and positioned it inside behind the opened front door, and my mom and I walked out with dad lingering behind. Scooter started yelling that I tried to rob him earlier in the day and he would have his revenge. I tried to explain what I did not say to him: "How much do you have on you?" What I said was, "How much did you get?" referring to their booty from robbing the Chinese laundry. Scooter [*hour we too see sense*] was refusing to accept my explanation. My dad started saying that he wanted them away from the front of his property. When my mom tried to reason with Scooter, defending me by saying I do not rob or steal from people, Scooter said something foul insulting my mother. It was too late for him then! I jumped over our gate and began whipping his ass thoroughly. As everyone stepped back to allow a fair fight, he had no answer to the fisticuffs I was putting on him. To avoid him any more embarrassment, his adult leaders stepped in and said, "That is enough." I reiterated what the misunderstanding was and apologized to Scooter for my initially approaching him, making it clear that the only reason I fought him was because of what he had said to my mother. We shook hands and all agreed that was the end of it. Soon Scooter and I became good friends as we both spent lots of time in and around the pool room. He became a master pool player and even offered me tips on the game, but I only had limited time to spend playing. Yet I started going to the less-crowded Randoms Billiard Room on Fulton Street near Nostrand Avenue. There I met Cicero Murphy the Black and great billiards and pool player. I would often go to Randoms and spend hours **racking balls for him** when he was practicing straight pool, and even more hours **watching** as he practiced billiards, an exciting pool game that only uses three balls on the table. Randoms Billiards was just up the street from the corner of Fulton and Nostrand where I bought my shoes and had some of my clothes tailor-made, my parents were no longer tailoring by then. On the one corner was Florsheim's shoes, off the other corner was Stacey Adams, a few doors up from my tailor. Right around the corner from those stores and situated on Nostrand Avenue was a very exclusive Black culture—conscious and content-driven bookstore. There was another Black bookstore just like it on 125th Street in Harlem, from one of which I purchased the book *From Superman to Man* by R. A. Rogers.

That ninth-grade year was life changing for me. I had established myself in the neighborhood, had made male and female friends in my new neighborhood, experienced my introduction to blatant Black on Black bigotry, and it was the year of the New York City school boycott initiated to <u>integrate</u> [*rate game we tell in I / eat our girls . . . we Times enters I*] the city's high schools. And I believe that it was in the ninth grade that I took the National Aptitude Survey (NAS) and scored in the 97 percentile. I did not really know what percentile meant immediately. I understood later that it did not just mean that I was one of the high scorers on the test, but rather, it meant that of all the students in the nation who had taken the test, I scored higher than 97 percent of them. I was in the top three percent in aptitude, that is, natural ability to acquire any skill. I learned that one of my boxing idols, Floyd Patterson, who I would eventually meet in upstate New York and have a great conversation with after he retired, had grown up on Lexington Avenue which was a parallel street one block over from my house. I started going to Saturday night dances at the "Y" and watching track practice at the boys high school, learning to swim at the Y, hanging out with my intellectual friend Clayton O from Panama. Our favorite pastime was playing chess and playing "chest," blocking while trying to punch one another in the chest to see how fast we could punch, emulating Emile Griffin. (I seem to recall watching the tragic Benny "Kid" Piret versus Emile Griffin fight live around that time.)

I recall that there were several uppity-acting Black families on my block. They stood out because they were very light skinned and the girl and the others in her own family wanted everyone on the block to know that she was a student at Howard University [*Why "it" seen few I enter . . . you do war open head!*]. I was given the distinct impression that Howard U was where the better-than-thou uppity light-skinned Black students attended college. I was friendly with light-skinned Cheryl (she and I became lovers some years later), but I really loved light-skinned Diane A and she really loved me. There were two other light-skinned boys on the block that liked Diane, and she would hang out with the three of us. However, the other two boys would be invited into her house when her father, an NYC cop, was home, but he would literally block me from ever entering his house. I was too dark skinned. She and I discussed her dad's attitude. She made me feel like it truly did not matter, because his feelings did not change how she felt about me. What is ironic though is when the NY Dodgers left Brooklyn for California and closed Ebbitt's Field [*field test it be {we is}=wise*], Diane's family moved to the exclusive apartments built on the grounds at that site; and she eventually had a baby there with a guy of my same dark complexion.

Sex Wit Already Made (Matrix)

At any rate, my ninth-grade year was the year of the NYC school boycott to integrate NYC high schools. I was introduced to the idea by my friend Clayton O, who at the time was freshmen class president at Boys High School. He approached me and told me that he wanted me to be the representative at my junior high school, to encourage students at my grade level to be willing to attend a white high school upon graduation. To that end, he told me that he had been approached by Malcolm X and wanted me to come with him and participate in a meeting with Malcolm and other civil rights leaders at Rev. Milton Galamison's Shiloam Presbyterian Church over past Nostrand Avenue and on *Jefferson Avenue* between Fulton Street and Atlantic Avenue. I was delighted and honored to be asked to attend with him. Since Clayton was such a brilliant guy and Malcolm X was so important, I felt like I was being invited to the big times, that I somehow had attained a higher-class status when he invited me, because I realized then that he saw something in me that I had not yet fully recognized in myself until that time. And I would soon discover that *status consciousness* was true. When we arrived and entered the church, we walked toward the main sanctuary, and passing a side room, I looked in and beheld Malcolm X [*sex mine look out . . . see life already made*] centered to the doorway under bright lights in a gray suit being interviewed by reporters who really appeared enthralled by him. The way Malcolm was seated made it seem like he was picture-framed by the doorway; and it was as if he was looking directly at me. It was then that I noticed something about him that I had never noticed before then, and that is that he had red hair, more red than brown reddish-brown hair. I also met other big names there that day: Dick Gregory [*women ours out got we are game dick*], Percy Sutton [on time touch us women see our *we power*] (Malcolm's lawyer), Gordon Parks [*senses kept rap enters do hours go*] (*Time/Life* photographer), Ozzie Davis and Ruby Dee [*wee-wee did women rub down in area . . . is found already done . . . we I scheme is out*], Oscar Brown Jr. and his wife [wife is head down in area . . . ours joke . . . own ours be scar out], and others. (It was around

43

this time that I remember Ossie Davis making the statement: Those who know don't tell, those who tell don't know! In later years, I would develop personal acquaintances with Gordon Parks, Dick Gregory, and Oscar Brown Jr. I would meet and have discussions with Gordon Parks at his Time/Life office in Manhattan. I escorted Dick Gregory to the <u>Westwood Ho Hotel</u> [*Licks we tell out . . . head hood out . . . words rest*] on Central Avenue in Phoenix, Arizona, after a concert that he gave at <u>Arizona State University</u> [*women "it" some . . . few I into . . . you eat stuff . . . already no / know (now kept) scheme air*], when he was still doing a comedy act. By then I was a full-time student at ASU and a Tempe police officer (and all unbeknownst to him I had appointed myself his bodyguard). He invited my two friends and I, who rode with us when I drove him to his hotel and escorted him to his room. There we spent a couple of hours with him laughing until our sides ached, as he just casually made conversation. He was a natural comedian. Just about everything that came out of his mouth was hilarious when he was in comedy mode intellectually. By the time I got to the University of California at Berkeley as a graduate student, Oscar Brown Jr. and his wife would frequent a club that I frequented, so we reunited our acquaintance there and Oscar would sometimes perform the slave auction song ["Bid 'em in get 'em in"] and others.)

There were speeches made that day I first met Malcolm, and serious discussions over several days following. Malcolm gave my friend Clayton his handwritten speech of that day. In a private meeting after the speeches, Malcolm gave me instructions on what he would like me to follow up on at my school, recruit students at my school who would be willing attend Erasmus Hall or Fort Hamilton high school upon graduation. I do not remember the context, but I recall Malcolm telling me that I needed to do two things: look up the definition of Negro in the first edition of the Americana encyclopedia/dictionary and also to read the book *What the Egyptians Knew* [ways we in kept answers . . . tip . . . game {we mind already given} eye thoughts after

44

head works / new kept answers: I took pussy women gave . . . wee-wee thoughts after head (ad he) worked / news kept answers . . . pen do . . . is it, women egg . . . thoughts after head worked]. Over the years, I had searched near and far and never found a record of the book, and now I know that book may never have needed to exist, because its implied potential content is clear. However, I recently discovered that there was a book published in 1964 entitled _The Egyptian's Knew_ by Tillie S. Pine. My discussion with Malcolm predated this book's publication, so it is doubtful he could have been referencing it. No matter, early on I had found several first addition dictionaries with the 7-point definition of a Negro. Points like, they smell like hircine (goat), they have arms that extend below the knee pan, they have exceedingly thick craniums enabling them to use the head as a weapon of attack, and they come in different shades of dark skin from black to blue black.

The boycott happened, and were it not for his two bodyguards, I would have stood directly beside Malcolm X across the street from the board of education headquarters in downtown Brooklyn, Jay Street Borough Hall section, during the boycott, and I was among the approx. fourteen students from Sands Junior High School who signed up for and upon graduation attended a predominantly white high school; when I for one could have attended the Boys High School. A _"fly"_ predominantly Black high school within walking distance from my house. Instead, I attended Fort Hamilton High School [_cool shush head given I have not liked . . . I made ahead time for_] which was an hour and a half by combination of train and bus each way from my house. Yes, three-hour transit to and from school-on-school days. The way we kept in touch with the rest of the Sands Junior High School group that attended other white high schools around Brooklyn is that we would meet at the roller rink on Empire Boulevard on Friday nights and skate to the latest dance music. On other weekend nights, we would meet in the **"city,"** Manhattan, at The Dom [_mind overdue he thinks_] disco for shows or just for dancing. I remember a special night of fun I was having dancing with a beautiful girl to the Jimmy Castor band's music while there.

I do not recall all the other intricacies that went into my participation in the boycott, but I do recall Malcolm opening the Shabazz restaurant [want you already straight . . . wee hours scheme is . . . already bitch has] on Bedford Avenue between Fulton Street and Atlantic Avenue down from the large national guard armory. For me it was all about bean pies then. The idea that a pie made of beans tasted as good as, if not better than, sweet potatoes pie was a phenomenon to me at the time. Lucky for me that I at least tasted the bean pie early on, unlike what I had done with cheesecake. I had refused to ever taste cheesecake when it was offered to me. And it was not until I was a full-grown adult, before I accidentally discovered it did not taste like cheese. Now how obtuse is that?!

While I did not choose to join the Black Muslims, in the days when I would attend Malcolm's speeches on Sunday evenings at the mosque on Bedford Avenue a few short blocks, within two hundred yards, of my house. However, I had been considering joining his Organization for African American Unity. In that regard, my last effort to be involved with Malcolm came on the day of his assassination. As I and my church-related best friend Philip H [hear lips hip] were crossing the street exiting from my house, on our way to catch a train to the *Audubon Ballroom* [*mind woo like lab. No, be idea you audition*] to hear Malcolm speak, my dad, who had become the pastor of our church by then, called to us announcing that Malcolm had just been shot. By the time we got back into the house to the TV screen, he was declared deceased. Earlier on I had developed a talking group big brother type of relation with Gordon Parks from our first time meeting up at the church. JFK and Malcolm's death had taken an emotional toll on me, so when I needed some where do we go from here kind of personal power cheer up talk, I would go over to Gordon Parks Time/Life building offices and have brief personally encouraging talks with him. In the three or four times that I visited him there, if he was in his office, he would always grant my visit and I was always respectful of his valuable time. If he was out of the office for the day, I would just cruise the diamond district and take a leisurely subway ride back home. I will never forget him for his relaxed, calming, wise counsel and genuinely friendly demeanor, despite his celebrated and renowned status.

Even before Malcolm's death and certainly since, my focus was on graduating from Fort Hamilton High School on time and with an academic college preparatory diploma. You see, the high school boycott was not about just attending school with white kids. It was primarily about competing with white kids academically and winning. Our private or small group conversations with the boycott leaders, including Malcolm, centered around whether each of us had the courage and academic confidence to successfully compete with whites in predominately white schools not knowing what the potential obstacles would be. Only those of us who felt we could and should meet that existing challenge elected to participate. Fearlessly achieving academic success was the goal. In the interim, I maintained the honor role in mathematics and typing. And I can affirm that to the person, every student from Sands JHS that went to Fort Hamilton HS graduated on time and we attended our Brooklyn College graduation ceremony together. For logistical reasons, I did not attend our high school prom which was held at the Waldorf Astoria Hotel in Manhattan. Moreover, I only had two fights in high school. (My last fight in junior HS, when I was still kind of aggressive, was with Roscoe J. I remember it because we had been friends and were kind of evenly matched in terms of bravado, but he was taller than I. We fought toe to toe for about an hour standing up under the BQE overpass across the street from Sands and punching for so long that my partner, Sumner L, asked me, "Aren't you ready to stop?" And I replied, "I'm not stopping until I draw blood." And I did not stop fighting until that happened, because that was my only way to demonstrate that I won the fight. Yet there is another reason that I am reminded of that fight. I used to hang out a lot all over Manhattan on the weekends. Once, and I do mean once, I entered one of the sleezy movie theaters on Forty-second Street near Broadway. The storyline of the film was about a detective trying to solve a crime and needing to question a lot of active prostitutes in the process. Opportunistically [why *call it sin? I into you . . . time hour . . . offer penis . . . pussy opens*], he would make up reasons to have sexual intercourse with some of the prostitutes under the guise of pursuing the investigation. In the one scene, he is having continuous sex with a prostitute that he liked and was thrusting in and out so long that she was to the point of exhaustion, so she asked him, "When are you going to stop?" And he replied, *"I'm not stopping until I get to the bottom of this!"* As it turned out, it was one of the funniest movies I have ever seen!

Anyway, my best friend Sumner L. was the captain of the hall monitors at my high school, and he hired me to man a post on my floor. He had become thoroughly religious by this time and had just been at my post telling me the virtues of how the Scriptures said we should turn the other cheek when offended. It was only a few minutes after Sumner left my post that a male student came from an exit and wanted to enter the restroom. I asked him for his pass, and he pushed me and walked on into the restroom. I followed him into the restroom and insisted that he show me his hall pass, at which point he smacked me in my face. Then he went to swing at me, and I flipped him down onto the urinal and proceeded to slam his head on the urinal, as Sumner L. luckily returned and rescued him. Afterward Sumner chided me, he knew I was a fighter, I thought I had just finished talking to you about turning the other cheek. I explained to him that the guy had pushed me, then he slapped me. And that was the equivalent of both cheeks. I only have two cheeks, so when he tried to hit me again, I had no other option but to light his ass up. Sumner and I went way back, and I had the highest respect for him. He was still living in the Farragut housing projects when we attended high school together. It was Sumner L., who approached me at that same hall monitoring post and informed me that JFK had been killed, even before students were summoned to our homerooms and the principal making the formal announcement and releasing us from school. That sad day, I witnessed grown men openly and shamelessly crying on the buses and in the subways during what must have been my longest ride home.

Meanwhile, when at home on Quincy Street between my graduation from junior high school and my HS graduation at seventeen, a lot of social activity and growth different from my project experiences had taken place. In addition to friends that I made on my block, I started spending a lot of time in Manhattan on the weekends with two siblings, Philip and Paul, who were members of my church. We spent time in the Village and Washington Square Park, at Central Park events, in Harlem, and on Delancey Street, among other things. I spent lots of time at home studying, taking care of my Guppy fish tank, playing stick ball in the street, walking down to Classen-Dekalb Avenue Park near Pratt Institute and behind the police station to play handball. When Connie Hawkins was suspended from the NBA, I used to retrieve the basketball for him on misses, as he practiced shooting in that same park during breaks between handball matches, I regularly played at that park. I believe that was the schoolyard of P.S. 258. I had my girlfriend, Helen, who lived around the corner on Lexington Avenue to entertain and attend dances with at the Y. When I look back, I wonder how I found the time to do all the things that I involved myself with, but I did. I even spent many hours just sitting on my stoop with friends and neighbors just "people watching." Quincy was a city bus route, so the street stayed busy. A lot of the activity related to drug trafficking around the corner at the pool room. Over time I watched many normal acting new faces, male and female, go from handsome or beautiful to heroin-laced nodding and bumming on the street corner. It was a pitiful sight. I witnessed a knife fight between two men in front of my house as I sat on my stoop, and a woman stabbing a man in front of my stoop as they casually talked about her continually stabbing him as they walked down the street. I also witnessed a woman beating a man so severely with her purse that he crawled under a car to safety. Once as I was sitting in my house during the early morning before noon, I began hearing gunshots coming from the vacant lot on Gates Avenue directly in back of my house. I crawled into the kitchen and peeped out in time to see a Black man on one knee firing at a blond-headed white cop firing back from the cover of his police vehicle. Just then, as the Black gunman stood up and began firing with a gun in each hand a bullet crashed through our kitchen window. I ducked down and crawled back into our living room. Then I heard a few shots coming from the Quincy [*women see enter I you question*] street side of the house, so I stayed down. Within five minutes, my sister came knocking at our front door telling me to come out and see what was going on. What I observed was a blooded Black man in handcuffs walking in a defiant bebop style, looking around at the crowd that had gathered, as he moved toward a police car. The bridge of his nose appeared to be shot through, one kneecap appeared to be shot through and hanging down, and he had what appeared to be bullet holes in both arms and one shoulder. He was placed in a police car and driven away. But the story did not end there. He went on to escape from the hospital when they got him there. And he was not recaptured until three months later, after running a red light in Harlem [*mind we look hours ahead*]. He came to be known as the Brooklyn Bicycle Bandit [*time ideas ban cycle. I be into women looking kept open bar*]. He had been shot five times that day, and when asked how he healed himself, he said that he used Mercuro-Chrome [*we made options our choice cure opens our minds*].

I did not decide to go to college until December of my senior year in HS. Prior to that time, my plan, along with Sumner L. believe it or not, and a few others of my buddies from my former housing projects were planning to join the Green Beret, and go fight in Viet

Nam. I already had two of my first cousins over there, who would eventually be lost over there, and I had fallen for the hubris in the propaganda song "The Ballard of the Green Beret." However, my good friend Clayton O. had begun attending SUNY, Albany, starting in September of my senior year, and I became open to more critical thinking about what to do with myself upon graduation. Additionally, I knew that my friend Allen B., who I had known since we lived on the same floor in the projects on Sand Street and who was then playing starter basketball for Boys HS, had gotten a full scholarship to play for the, University of Tulsa, in <u>Tulsa, Oklahoma</u> [already *made offered ad he . . . already kept looking . . . often already seen . . . like . . . you talk*]. Consequently, attending a college away from home became a central idea to me. I knew I would be leaving my HS girlfriend behind, but our relationship was marginal at best, and I could see her when I came home for Christmas and during summer vacation. Then came the thought of choosing schools to apply to. I would not choose Tulsa, because Allen and I would be into partying too much. He would be a girl magnet. Then I stumbled on an article in *Time* magazine extolling the great climate and wonderous living in Arizona. It just so happened that my track idol Henry Carr, from the 1964 Olympic world record 4x400 relay team and 200-meter gold medalist, attended Arizona State University, so my college preference top choice was made. I went on to apply to ASU, the University of Illinois at Carbondale, and the University of Michigan at Ann Arbor. The first school that I heard back from in April of my senior year was my first choice, ASU, and it was an acceptance letter. To this day, I cannot tell you what the status of my other two applications were, because if they came, I never paid attention to them, being so elated knowing I would be going to the school of my choice. Prior to receiving the acceptance letter, I had not mentioned much of anything to my parents about what I had been considering. They knew that Clayton O. had gone away to college, and I was pondering what to do in my own life. I had been working part-time as a stock clerk at a cosmetic supply store after school and one overnight on weekends at my uncle's "hack" station <u>cleaning</u> [*gotten in I learned see*] and parking yellow cabs. My uncle was a master mechanic who could remove, take apart, rebuild, and replace a <u>transmission</u> [*mission answers our times*] in a single night's shift. He worked for a Jewish hack station owner named Hymie. His worked kept Hymie's yellow cabs on the road, and Hymie became one of the largest medallioned yellow cab company owners in NYC. My uncle was still living on Amsterdam Avenue when he retired, so Hymie bought him a house in the Bronx near the original Yankee stadium.

I had no tangible idea of how I would finance my education other than an initial $750 from NYS education <u>fund</u> [*due fun*]; but when I received the acceptance letter in April, I went to my mom and simply said to her that I would be moving to Arizona in September to attend college. My parents immediately rallied in my support, and my dad and I even flew out to <u>Phoenix</u> [*sex I into hoe purpose*] in early August to scout out <u>Tempe</u> [*we pubic me touch*]. Together we met members of the freshmen football team players who would turn out to be my adopted new family. We would all be making our way far away from our homes and family. There is a lot that I could unpack here, but I will simply say that student work study jobs, establishing state residency, several major full and part-time jobs, and dropping out of school for a full year to work and save money to finance my tuition and loans enabled me to graduate with a bachelor's degree in mathematics after six years. Not so bad, because for the average student graduating from a four-year college in exactly four years is typically a joke anyway. Yes, I changed my major from engineering technology to a mathematics science major during my first year, because all the labs associated with the classes in engineering science did not allow me any time to spend with my local family, the athletes. I seriously doubt that my parents could have been aware, as I was unaware at the time, that the NAS [national aptitude survey] test had labeled me an *"it"* [*target I*]. It had been established that I had brains, some academic prowess, and a thirst for knowledge, so my life habits, moral behavior, and academic progress would all be subject to continuous scrutiny. All for the most obvious of reasons: a type of *social behavioral observation* a.k.a. *social control.* These are all afterthoughts, and there was one thing that stood out and let me know that my major challenge would be in academics, was the sudden appearance and use by most other students of the slide ruler in my math-related classes. I had been in the honor role in math in HS, and I was in the college preparatory sequence of classes; but not once did anyone ever even mention a slide ruler much less teach how to use a slide ruler. When I started my predominantly white student-filled classes at ASU in electrical technology within the engineering department, most of the students used a slide ruler to perform calculations. That one specific observation of the **covert** reach of white students academically and their predetermined focused skills set **steeled** me for the journey ahead. I was to be out to "sea" [*all we seen/ sensed*] in the Michele Foucault conception of the term. To persevere, I would unwittingly be exposing myself to the subtle extremes of what Foucault called "Madness and Civilization" [*No, I after scheme. I looked, I found I see. Sin seen we into defiled a man*]. Good thing for me I had mastered arithmetic [see times thought air / see I met head wit already] in the fifth grade and had *dexterity* [*women* wit we talk/tell sex we did] performing numerical calculations. I never did take the time to learn how to use a slide ruler. No matter, Texas Instruments [*crooked men you are . . . time, sin, taxes*] calculators have rendered slide rulers superfluous. However, had I continued as an electrical technology student, I would likely have become a multimillionaire by now. Being a first-generation college student in my family, I did not know any better, and consequently, there was no informed person close enough to guide me. Not only was ASU one of the top engineering schools in the nation at the time, but I used to routinely play black/hard ball handball with one of the top handball players in the country on the courts behind Saharo Hall dormitory. He was by coincidence [*we see in . . . we "I do" seed coin*] also one of the chief engineers working on the development of the cell phone for Motorola in Phoenix. Back in the engineering department, I maintained a student work-study job where I did all of the calibration work; on the soil testing an engineer was doing to develop an enzyme [*me why scheme*] entered additive to arrest some of the bacteria and <u>solidify</u> [*women found I lid so*] the soil at the construction sites of the 1968 Mexico City Olympic Games. The odd thing is the engineer that I worked on the project with and who had <u>successfully</u> [*Why? Looks like you found something . . . scene we see is you suicide*] developed a suitable enzyme ending my work with him, went into his office a few days later, and committed suicide. Again, you cannot make these things up!

This last <u>anecdote</u> [*dote sees we enter areas*] reminds me of how much more I could have unpacked regarding my experiences leading up to undergraduate school. I chose not to because I only wanted to present just some of the essence of my background. However, as I reflect on it now, there are a few more things I should mention because of their significance in my life. That is, after moving into the projects in Brooklyn, my family went from my parents joining a church, to my dad becoming a deacon and my mom an usher and choir lead singer, on to my dad being ordained a minister, my sister and I becoming lead singers in the junior choir, and finally my dad pastoring that same *<u>church</u>* [*choice ours you chose*], after Rev. Jethro's passing, for nineteen years. That meant I attended Sunday school and the main church service virtually every Sunday until I left New York at seventeen. My mom was a kind and gentle person, and she was one of the best cooks that I will ever know. My dad was rough on the edges but loved the church and cared for others. He once gave away our family car to the previous pastor, because that pastor had six or seven kids and lived farther away from the church than we did. So the four of us went from driving to church to riding the city bus to church. It took me years to appreciate the sacrifice my parents made then and to forgive my dad for it. By the way, that model car in its original green color is today a classic and worth hundreds of thousands of dollars.

There are many more intriguing stories and anecdotes that I could share with you regarding my personal life experiences. For example, I could involve you in the intimacies and learning experiences I encountered living in and attending colleges in Arizona and California, or similarly my unique adventures living in California, Atlanta, and back again in New York. However, this treatise is not simply autobiographical. I have used some of my personal life experiences—opportunely—to randomly select and cipher arbitrary literary items, as an objective sampling of what can be revealed in the **transcript** of an individual's life, through the lens of cryptographic interpretation of text. The things that I uncovered in these samplings, as content, were as new to me as they currently are to you. The things that are revealed as I do this work has given my work incentive. Learning truths about life is my least fear. Truth and clarity of thought energizes me. Consequently, I have a justification for moving forward. (As to you—*readers*—you might want to hold on to your metaphorical seat belts.) I will now exit from my personal story and focus our attention on the target project. That is, the cryptographic unpacking of some of the meaning *inherent* in the early parts of the written text in the book of <u>Genesis</u> [*is* genes / sis we enter we gain] from the KJV of the Scriptures.

Chapter Two

Do You Want To Hear About It?

I have read the King James Version of the Scriptures from cover to cover at least twice, but I had never really studied it with _discernment_ [time men enter hours . . . we see sense . . . I did]. My only concern had been to expose myself adequately to its overall content, because, from my youth, I had been frequently hearing people quoting from the Scriptures as plug-ins for thought. Moreover, I have always been troubled by several "archetypes" in my head concerning the creation of man. The one was that God began humankind from just a single male-female couple and their great initial sin was eating an _apple_ from a tree that some mysterious third entity had suggested they could eat from without consequences, despite God's directive that they not do so. The primary paradox in my mind was if all of mankind started with a single couple, a lot of _incest_ had to have gone on in the aftermath. The fact that this so-called cardinal sin was _inevitably_ in the mix was also an enigma to me. Therefore, I recently assigned myself to at least explore what the book of Genesis has definitively to say about it all. Especially since the Scriptures are a _primary_ source for the knowledge of sin.

When I began, I wanted first to determine whether I was reading pure allegory or a cipher. When manually doing a content analysis of literary text, the work can be extraordinarily difficult. Consequently, I have learned to look for a "hook" first before I dive in. A hook informs me that the proximate literary text being read is encrypted. That a very deep insight is immediately being made available. I found my answer as an embedded "hook," that fixed my literary gaze in the statement: "and closed up the flesh instead thereof" (Gen. 2:21). The expression "instead thereof" literally means *"alternative to 'that' or 'it.'"* These two words represent a hook, because they have a curious *contextual* [look around you text on sees] placement; and, given that these are a set of words (*that* and *it*) which when taken together represent a unique cryptographic signification. What a hook does is it lets you know that the literary form you are examining is designed to be an immediate *interplay of, on, and with words.* A secret or hidden script. A type of "*crosswords puzzles*" [seen we life scheme is you put words cross] I knew then that I was reading a cryptograph. The young woman Toby from "Tibees" on YouTube, in her discussion of the famous mathematician Alan Turing cites the book ***Mathematical Recreations and Essays***, which provides the following excellent definitions of the words *cryptograph* and *cipher.*

A ***cryptograph*** may be defined as a manner of writing in which the letters or symbols employed are used in their natural sense but are so arranged that the communication is intelligible only to those possessing a key. A ***cipher*** may be defined as a manner of writing by characters arbitrarily invented or by an arbitrary use of letters, words, or characters in other than their ordinary sense intelligible only to those possessing a key.

Having stumbled onto a hook, I returned to the first verse of Genesis to begin my discernment work using a keyed cipher. The subsequent narrative will explain what was revealed. Reminding you that unpacking cryptographic material is difficult, I will have to limit some citations from within the text and require you to simply ***beg the question***. *That is, assume that what I am saying is true.* In addition, I limited the text that *I* unpack basically to the first four chapters of Genesis, St. John 1:1–5, and Hebrew 4:12. Yet I was encouraged to add a very few additional miscellaneous but relevant scriptures. Overall, the limited scriptural text that I have reviewed has been sufficient in answering all my earlier questions regarding creation. As for me, it has also helped to put traditional scriptural interpretation onto a larger more realistic and practical contextual plain. Moreover, one must always remind themselves that *any* knowledge that we *seek* was already available before we came on the scene, so to speak. The knowledge that we gain is only by the grace of God, which his Holy Spirit has assisted us in obtaining. We must first understand that God's words are in "double-speak." In each statement, God's words are referring to the physical world and the spiritual world at the exact same time. That is, there are layers of meaning that necessarily overlap when his words are transcribed. Thus, his words relate facts of science and mysticism "simultaneously" [sly you out . . . neat {eat no} . . . like you I am seen]. In its more rigorous form, this is what modern-day physicists call "quantum entanglements." That is, as by my own emphasis, quantum "word" entanglements. It is what Albert Einstein referred to as "spooky action at a distance." They are complexities of thought which make up what life and reality truly is. Consequently, I am obliged to *stipulate* that the Scriptures are divinely written. That is, they are written by individuals who were in touch with and inspired by historical and *spiritual* reality. In fact, the scriptures are a cryptograph, and this observation remains true even if, as many argue, the scriptures are missing some of their original text. Missing portions of text does not prevent us from ciphering the existing text, for its immediate content.

Since in the process of learning, paying close attention to definitions is of the utmost importance; let me attempt a sound bite on what God is to me, before I discuss some of the earliest content in the book of Genesis. My spiritual notion of God [The Creation Spirit] is as follows:

God is an all-powerful united plurality of *thinking* spirit. The most powerful and single force of energetic thought comprised of precise words, which combine to have spoken things into existence in all their preordained complexities, even *before they will eventually* be made to appear.

Although easily uttered, what I just stated is not easily comprehended, much less believed by the everyday person. The Scriptures tells us (John 1:1–5):

In the beginning was the Word, and the Word was with God, and the Word was God. *The same was in the beginning with God* [*Do game* heads wit. Game in I entered. Begin we hint saw we man as *we thoughts*]. All things were made by him, and without him was not anything made that was made. In him was life, and the life was the light of men. And the light shineth in darkness; *and the darkness comprehended it not* [*Time* on *"it"* ended he are comp(rehended). Sin seen we entered *dark* {kept hours already done}; *we thoughts* done entered *all*].

Thus, the book of Genesis [is sin gene / sin is gene] begins: **In the beginning God** {The Creation Spirit} **created the heaven and the earth.** Period! God simply imagined and then spoke creation and its aftermath into existence. For a believer and all those who understand who and what God is, I do not think anything more need be said. Because you appreciate what a complex of reality God is. What God speaks into existence *materializes* completely within *its* own time. ***Creation and*** all that followed with the dual and simultaneous phenomenon of ***procreation*** in mankind. Within his creation, he *proposed* procreation. Procreation can be viewed as being embedded in creation as a necessary and sufficient condition for the continuity of mankind. Most ministries that I have listened to take for granted the implicit power that God ***bequeathed*** [does he eat you . . . question we be] **to man** to reproduce what God had originally uniquely made. Yet this is precisely what Genesis is written to highlight. More than man's creation itself, Genesis is really focused on the intricacies of procreation as it relates to mankind's immediate and subsequent behavior, once they were placed on this *planet* [times . . . "we" plan].

What the Scriptures are explaining early on are the thoughts of God. As such it is written as *double-entendre.* The words necessarily have dual usages and meanings, because God is referring to both the spiritual world and the physical world simultaneously; as he reveals some of his workings of creation and his intentions, along with the consequential *behavior* [hour opened I founded ahead . . . we be] of mankind. As incredible as it may sound, under a double-entendre, one is being told at least two things at the exact same time. The facts then necessarily appear very *compressed,* so they take some hard work, very focused effort, to untangle. Let us also recognize that literally, by definition, **double-entendre** speaks to the **risqué** and **indecent** in human speech and activity. Both are inherent in the current contexts along with the occurrence of or application *of pun* [into you put / enter you people], as a play on words view.

Especially when reading the scriptures, the reader must understand and adopt a unique perspective. A parallax view towards what they are reading. That is, the writers of the scriptures are not using their own design or even their desired words in some cases. They are using God's words as he is divining them to be scripted. And God is not talking to himself, he is talking to us, in his words, and speaking of other groups of males and females whom he had created and placed on the planet together with his cast of characters: Adam, Eve, the Serpent, Cain, and Abel. He uses the cast to demonstrate to his chosen observers how he originally made the first group of males and females to make clear what he purposed for them, procreation. He needed then to purpose "sin" as the "germ" of procreation, to explain all the ramifications of the act of procreation. Why? Because human beings do not construct beings in the same way that God originally did. Although our construction method is qualitatively different, our result in physical "children" is equivalent, in both form and content, to what God designed. By augmenting the concept of "sin," God was able to teach man the nature of "thought" and "critical thinking." So that man would have all the tools needed to build and "replenish" the planet.

Before I go deeper into the cipher, I need to highlight some things that most people would take for granted. I will list them axiomatically:

- The beasts referenced in the first chapter of Genesis were placed on the planet before man. As a result, the word "day" and the concept of "time" necessarily lose their conventional meanings and take on contextual meanings. Thus, the evidence opens to both evolutionists and creationist views of events to have occurred in space and time as is evidenced by fossilized dinosaurs.
- God spoke directly to most of the original cast of characters separately, i.e., Adam, Eve, the Serpent, and Cain. He did not speak with Abel, which hints of simulation.
- God did not have to place the serpent and the two special trees [see our time] in the garden along with the male and female, but he did!
- God does not appear to have been a constant presence in the garden.
- When the man and woman realized that were naked, they first clothed themselves in "sewed fig leaves" (Gen. 3:7), and later God clothed them in "coats of skins" (Gen. 3:21).
- The male could see the difference and had a visceral reaction at the first sight of the female (Gen. 2:23).
- The fact that the word "woman" appears in the text before the man called it out (Gen. 2:22) is significant. It suggests that God put the names of all the animals and the potential for all language in the man's head as well, ahead of time, when breathing in the "breathe of life," the set of all words that will ever enter the minds of mankind.

- God speaks double-speak, so there is "density" in the composition of his words and their comprehension. Thus, we find thought and afterthought in understanding.
- The male and female are introduced as fully grown adults, not enfants.
- As represented in the Scriptures, Cain was the FIRST naturally birthed CHILD, as illustration.
- The woman and the serpent loved each other. So much so that God had to force "enmity" between them. In the same sentence, he put enmity between the seed of the women and the seed of the serpent. Within context, for those respective seeds to have had such a significant *relation*, they would have had to have a common maternity, the same mother. Moreover, and in the same sentence, the text alludes to the respective "seeds" having a conflict between themselves (Gen. 3:15).
- God had to command the woman to submit to her "husband" [do ban sin you head] . . . Adam (Gen. 3:16).
- God reveals on a need-to-know basis, and this is when "time" and perhaps even "place" has relevance.
- God at one point "cursed" Cain, then changed his mind, and instead protected and blessed him. Why? (Gen. 4:11–17).
- God made mention of the woman's "seed" and the serpent's "seed" in the same sentence. Within context, this suggests that Cain was the offspring of the woman and the serpent and implies that Abel was the first offspring of Adam and Eve.
- We are all a part of God's *simulation* [in (awake) out (asleep) I target all "like" (meaning exactly the same) you meant I sensed]. As individuals, we can walk down the road of our individual lives, as well as we "choose" to, by being open to God unveiling what you allow yourself to receive. Understanding that your personal growth in the world impacts every other living thing on the planet. That is, our words and deeds matter. Of course, our words all belong to God. He has literally given them to us.

The words belonging to God that you use are the data defining your levels of both worldly and spiritual consciousness. It is a multiplex of meanings. Sometimes those words appear raw to our sensibilities, but they all have essential substance in God's word realm of quantum entanglements. God created mankind out of his thoughts, imbuing us with the apparatus to procreate and learn how to think for our self, with help from his living Holy Spirit. In fact, the entire scenario outlined in the second through the fourth chapters of Genesis is purposed by God to hardwire into to us the insight and jump start our ability to *think critically* when attempting to resolve the riddles of life. This is what is meant by whatever you "loose on earth will be loosed in heaven" (Mat. 16: 19 and Mat. 18:18). God has opened unlimited possibilities for mankind. Only our choices and time limit us. Within these contexts and according to Scriptures, LGBTQIA+, for example, is nothing less than the self-chosen alphabet of defiant or perverted sexual behavior. God has given us the ability to understand "anything," but we cannot "know," as only God can and does know, everything. God created the world! He does not have to micromanage it. God made our reality to be self-actualizing.

Now let me make clear what a cipher of the text is offering the reader by way of content in the first four chapters of Genesis. First and foremost, I noticed (discovered), within this scriptural context, the following words are used *synonymously* and *interchangeably:* man; Adam; male-female; heaven-earth; tree yielding seed-herb bearing seed; seed-herb; lesser light-greater light; image-likeness; good-evil; fruitful-multiply; and night-day. In each of these expressions, God is referring to his *dichotomy* of male and female, period. This is a matter of fact! Simply put, in the cipher and in the ordered-relations as I have listed them, male then female, each of these expressions provides a unique *"characterization"* of the respective gender types. God wanted it to be *unequivocally* clear that the male and the female were made as unique and distinct entities. Male as contrasted with female is the context in which these expressions are being applied, beginning in chapter 1. I had considered delineating each of the characteristics individually, but quite frankly, doing so would reveal too precise information about my key, so I abandoned the idea.

Another idea implied in chapter 1 is that when God created man, he created many individuals of both genders, but they were essentially docile, did not know their *butts from a hole in the ground, so to speak.* Although God had mentioned in chapter 1 that after him, they would reproduce their kind in their image by combining the male and female seed given naturally to each of them; they did not even recognize that they were naked, much less know how to go about procreating. Hence, God literally had to teach them how to start "thinking." In other words, God initially built man as an innocent non-thinking fully grown adult, not a physical infant. Consequently, the text in chapter 2 has God demonstrating how he first made them distinct yet having a physical means of connection. Then in order to activate their thinking, since there had been no observable prior experience that they shared or could draw from, for they had not grown up being taught by any significant others, God had to *purpose* sin! As a matter of fact, based on the written text! As quiet as it is kept, God purposed sin to introduce man to <u>*critical*</u> thinking [get into I ink thoughts. Look around . . . I wit sees.]. God <u>*figuratively*</u> [women lips . . . we find it all. Hour <u>*you*</u> {you opened women} game . . . I found], excuse the pun, *"ribbed"* or *"teased"* man into learning to <u>*think critically*</u> [women living life already see "it." I hours see inks thoughts]. By the way, in order to really appreciate creation, one had to suspend their convention notion of time!

As the allegory depicts in chapter 2 of Genesis, God *demonstrated* how he made a male as distinct, in a different way, from how he made a female, so there would be absolutely no confusion. *Here, <u>I see what</u>*

you did not [time no ideas do you why after head works see I]. To better understand what is going on in the text of the Scripture, you have to imagine yourself and the other beings that God had already made seated in the gallery of a sterile *"operating theater"* [ours eat we thoughts ruining we power over/hours we after he thinks rating we power over] watching a surgery in an environment designed to prevent *"cross-contamination"* [nation I mean people before "no" sees *"cross" (double entendre . . . double-cross)*], where God is figuratively demonstrating how he made the male in comparison to how he made the female. The thought transferred is, "Ain't that a bitch" [Choice it be a afterthought time in I already (the "rib" taken from *inside* the man to make the woman)]. Used also as a pun, referring to God "teasing" man.

We are told that God first made the male *figure;* and afterward *"breathed into his nostrils* the breath of life (the reach of life or expanse of life); *and man became a living soul"* (Gen. 2:7) [Licks you out sin. Game in I found I live/evil already me already sees Be man down in area life found/falls out. Head eat be her *stuff* {first find you stupid}. *Lips I ours straight, No!* Since I must enter, I downed our heads. Eat ours bye.]. (If it is not clear to you what the cipher is explaining here, let me tell you in general terms. The thought is that cunnilingus is an insidious sin. If you find it out from the game, then it means you are alive. Babies fall out when men perform coitus with women. Straight men say no to cunnilingus, and they understand why not to do it, implying God views homosexuality as sin.). Bear with me, and I will explain more as we go along.

God then planted a beautiful garden and put the man in the garden along with several unique trees. One of which the man was told not to eat of it. It was the tree of the knowledge of good and evil [live down in area "do goo." Find we game know we thoughts. Found out wee-wee ours tricked. He thinks (saw it)!]. The text relates that God decided Adam needed a "help meet" [take wee-wee mind power {our we ways opens pussy} lick we head]. So God caused a "deep sleep" [pussy wee-wee licks same pussy wee-wee did] to fall upon Adam and he took one of his ribs and made a woman. Consequently, the cipher implies that God **"ribbed"** or **"teased"** Adam into behaving in a certain way, because taking a rib from Adam was merely symbolic of how God purposed sin. First by inducing a childlike reaction from both Adam and the woman, wherein, as a child, being told not to do something, would incite them to be even more eager to do it. If you are thinking that God did not **want Adam and the woman to eat that so-called "apple," think again.** As the Scripture informs us, God has said, "I make peace, and create evil: I the Lord do all these things" (Isaiah 45:6–7). Somethings may be good to you (lust) but not good for you (cunning). Thus, the necessary knowledge of **good** (do goo) and **evil** (live). Secondarily, by allowing the serpent to be present in the garden with Adam and the sensuous woman. To the woman, the serpent (present), who stood upright and spoke like a man; he was a Priapus (large penis) compared to the wee-wee (small penis) of Adam. (I use the term *Priapus* here because what the Scripture implies is more than just size and phallic symbol. It is referring to a thing symbolic of extreme or inordinate sexual desire and lust for pleasure.) How do we know that the serpent stood upright? He had had sex with the woman, and God did not dispatch him to the "ground" [wound game] until after those events took place. The woman and the serpent had become so smitten with each other that, after the fact, God had to put "enmity" between the woman and the serpent so that the woman could be made to bond with her husband, Adam (Gen. 3:15). The cipher of the text relates the serpent was more "subtil" [lips I tip . . . be you Sin!] (The serpent is naming the woman, Sin, here and suggesting she perform fellatio on him because he knew how she felt about him. Adam had named her "Woman" but the serpent called her "Sin" [internally {ally entering wet in I} I saw/was]. Obviously, and the cipher is clear, the woman committed adultery with the serpent, moreover Adam is likely to have observed. Doubtless, Adam was intimidated by the woman's ecstasy over the "Priapus." Thus, what was eaten in the garden was not the apple "fruit" ["it" (cunnilingus) you are found]. In this case we find the symbolic **apple** [we lick pussy penis areas]. (Let's see how much further we can take this thought. The following is the definition of an apple: <u>"the fruit of a tree of the genus Malus."</u> [seen you lips a male. Seen you enter we <u>games</u> {scent we males already got} We <u>thoughts</u> <u>(some taught head games you to hate). Found out wee-wee after ours.</u> <u>Find out "it" you ours heft</u>]. To be clear, these scriptures are talking about fellatio and cunnilingus. But we should not lose sight of the immediate purpose of these activities. God set it up, created the perfect environment, for these behaviors ("all me all see") using Adam, the woman, and the serpent, in view of the group of observers. They were learning how to procreate and how to think critically, in developing the discernment between good and evil issuing from sexual behavior and its relation to procreation. The cipher suggests the trio appeared surprised when Cain "fall before them" from the woman's womb as the progeny, I suspect of the woman and the serpent and not of Adam and the woman. As a matter of fact, I <u>believe</u> [Eve lie be] this is the reason Adam is said to have changed the woman's name to <u>Eve</u> [we found we] meaning not only that she was the first woman out of the other living females around to birth another human being, and to discover how it could forever be done. But it also suggests Adam's innocence, or naivety, in thinking it took the three of them—he, the woman, and the serpent—working together to give birth to the child. *The first fully human child.* What needs to be understood here is it is not likely that Adam previously had intercourse with the woman. He most likely only performed cunnilingus with the woman. He had at first witnessed the state of ecstasy the that the serpent brought the woman to (make it like it was) using his Priapus. God's present (=serpent) to the woman. Adam knew his wee-wee could not compete with the Priapus, so it is more likely that when the woman proffered him cunnilingus to bring her to an equivalent state of ecstasy as the serpent had "beguiled" [led I (Adam) you beg] her to do . . . he would eagerly have accepted (Gen.

3:13). Of course, this is only speculation on my part because I was not there, and this could have been a simulation, but it makes perfect sense within the scriptural context. Moreover, this scenario is the most likely since eating the **forbidden fruit** [it you . . . ours fine . . . end bid for] is the sin Adam did. Furthermore, we can be comfortable with this assessment of what happened because it is clear the woman was infatuated with the serpent (gift/present) and not Adam. And as it turned out, the serpent in agreement with the woman tricked Adam into performing cunnilingus on her precisely at a moment when Adam would ingest the live semen of the serpent, thus **defiling the** "man." In modern thought, the plot does not have to be so insidious in its purpose to defile a man. The mere submission to cunnilingus is considered to defile a man. In other words, the very possibility of a worst-case scenario, even as just an afterthought, is considered sufficient to defile a man.

Recall, God made the serpent and he initially stood upright and spoke like a man. And there was a consequence for the way that the woman and the serpent had treated Adam. For the scripture reveals God let the two of them know: "it"—what you have done—shall bruise thy "head"—the second child—and "thou" [you to hate] shall bruise "his"—the first child's—"heel" [lips wee-wee head] (Gen. 3:15–16). Notice that the second child, Abel, is referred to as the "head" and the first child from the woman, Cain, is referred to as the "heel," as person regarded with contempt or disproval. The reason for God making these distinctions will become clear when I later cipher the fascinating discussion that God and Cain have in the Scriptures regarding Abel. In the interim, I need to input some important additional information regarding cunnilingus.

The woman introduces the term "touch" in her conversation with serpent concerning what God had said regarding the *special* tree. (Remember now, the "tree of life" was also in the garden and theoretically God did not have to place either of the trees in the garden, if he did not choose to do so; but they each served an allegorical purpose in the text. For they did not "touch" the tree of life. We know this because God evicted them from the garden, Gen. 3:22–23, before that could take place). The woman stated that God had said not only not to eat of the tree but additionally "neither shall ye touch it" (Gen. 3:3). That is not what the Scriptures record God said to Adam, even before she was created from his "rib." Thus, on the face of it either she lied, it is what Adam related to her, or it is to serve an allegorical purpose. So the word *"touch"* [choice/choose out] has significance within this context, which is mainly because "touch" (sexually stimulating "touching" on or within the vagina) just happens to be the "alternative to" . . . "*that*" [*the* "afterthought" of the *potential harm* from cunnilingus] or "*it*" {"targeted I" using cunnilingus} . . . with respect to the conceptual act of defiling a man by using cunnilingus. Thus, the woman's introduction of the term "touch" was a "help," because symbolically the word completes a *trifecta* of our understanding surrounding the act of cunnilingus. As a poetic street saying once crudely explained it to me, "Pussy ain't nothing but meat on a bone . . . you can fuck it, suck it, or leave it alone.

Moreover, the text uses the word "woman" even before Adam uses it to label the nascent female (Gen. 2:22). Therefore, the term *"woman"* [man outweighed / out way] does not have the unique characterization Adam was supposed to have, implied by the text, attributed to it. As a result, we are presented with a logical **conundrum** [Man you are done . . . entered/into you (a strange male's semen) ended you enter *oversee*]. Thus, the idea of a male ingesting the semen of another male divests him of his God-given or divine position of power and of *oversight*. Which in turn and within context suggests the word *"pun"* [not you/ your people]. Continuing and following along this *reduction* we get **not you** (*you over women to end*) **people** [we *lips/licks pussy (submit* men) out we power. You offer women . . . Touch? No!]. The reference here again is to cunnilingus, which implies *cunning* and *lust* resulting in a male ingesting the **zygote** [we got women scheme] or **gametes** [set game

{**game tease we sin**}]. First suggesting that a male becomes a social pariah once he has submitted to or been subjugated to cunnilingus. That is, a woman's vagina being used as a repository and conduit for a *male* unwittingly ingesting the semen of another male. Which symbolically, if not actually, relegates that victimized male to the so-called "down low" in male sexuality, a means or form of homosexuality. Which is not only considered sinful but, when deliberately done illicitly, is criminal in my opinion. This, I suggest, is what took place given the woman's intimacy with the serpent when the scripture states: ***"She took of 'the fruit' ('it'. . . you her found time) thereof, and did eat, and gave also unto her husband with her; and he did eat"*** (Gen. 3:6). The woman knew that the serpent's semen was live (=evil) in her when she offered cunnilingus, repeatedly to her husband. And as to her part, she likely repeatedly performed fellatio on the serpent. In the end, it was God who made the woman *submit* to Adam as a committed wife: "And thy desire shall be to thy husband, and he shall rule over thee" (Gen. 3: 16).

My unpacking of this last quotation (taken from Gen. 3:6) should be instructive to you. Ciphered it reads: [Eat, did he?! Down in area?! Hours **he (the serpent)** head wit **her** husband to enter **you** also . . . **we (the woman and the serpent)** *"founded"* a *game* down in area. (When viewed intuitively, we even discover what the game was called. The game was called *"good for food"* [do opening find . . . hours opened . . . find do goo / do offense for do goo]). Eat did . . . done in area. Found out **we** her "touch" (choice **out**). **"It"** you ours fine "we head" time. Found (1) **"out"** [tongue you often] / (2) took "he" senses]. Thus, the second reason for the appellation "Eve" [we found we]. Here is also to be understood the context in which Genesis chapter one refers to the lesser [hour we less] (male) and greater [hour we eat our germs/gametes] (female) lights. Put simply, the woman was initially *made* smarter (cleverer . . . my emphasis) than the man.

The moralists refer to this behavior as a "sty" meaning debauchery. Legalists refer to the behavior as sodomy. Aware or "hip" street people call the behavior "it" [targeted I]. Lastly, a cryptographer would refer to the behavior as *"so"... meaning "out in the open" or "as a matter of fact."* No matter how we refer to the behavior, one must keep in mind God's purpose was the construction of a duality, *a lesser god.* God manufactured a lesser form of himself. *Figures that could think and equally could construct their own image and likenesses of themselves.* Think about the power in that! The power God gave to man. Also think about what exactly is "the knowledge of good and evil." It is the ability of *"critical thinking"* [game (we mean already get) into I ... Think (ink thought) let all ... see "it" ... I ours seeing]. This is the sensibility that God wants you to have while acknowledging that *"sin"* [entered I seen/scene] *is involved.*

Like the Scripture tells us: For the word of God is quick, and powerful, and sharper than any *two-edged sword* [*words* deed gets two/words education get educated over ways times], piercing even to the dividing asunder of *soul* and *spirit,* and of the *joints* and *marrow,* and is a discerner of the *thoughts* and *intents* of the heart (Heb. 4: 12).

Understand that the purpose and result of these actions was that God created man and taught man how to procreate and the sin that *accompanied* [die {we ideas} ends a plan mind oversees is already] it. Sin is the "by-product" of procreation, not the *"unintended consequence,"* because God knows exactly what he was and is doing!

One might argue, why not use a less, so-called "vulgar" term like vagina to express some of our delineations? Well what cipher do we get using for example the word *vagina* [already entering I (God/Word) got already found]?! In other words, every word that applies simply applies, notwithstanding one's opinion. We are looking at language objectively for meanings in textual materials without opinionating and bias. As needed, all words fall under God's purview. He is words! Albeit, for a variety of reasons, some words appear to be more appropriate than others, and at times are found to be more appropriate. However, it is important to note *language is a cosmos that oversees itself inside necessary and sufficient semantic connections. Words cannot be rigidly fixed in your mind; they are part of a flow. When using a cipher, <u>facts</u> [acts found] go from invisible to visible, without bias. Besides, being objective demands that one not be easily offended by one's own personal perceptions or by the opinions of others.*

Gen. 3:1–5: Concerning the discussion
between the woman and the serpent.

QUOTE

Now the serpent was more subtil than any beast of the field which the Lord God had made. And he said unto the woman, "Yea hath God said, 'Ye shall not eat of every tree of the garden?'" And the woman said unto the serpent, "We may eat of the fruit of the trees of the garden: But of the fruit of the tree, which is in the midst of the garden, God hath said, 'Ye shall not eat of it, neither shall ye touch it, lest ye die.'" And the serpent said unto the woman, "Ye shall not surely die. For God doth know that in the day ye eat thereof, then your eyes shall be opened, and ye shall be as gods, knowing good and evil." "(The alleged serpent does not lie to the woman here. He tells her the simple truth.)"

<u>Circuitous Interpretation</u>

To be clear, in my interpretations you are being given the gist of what is being said in the cipher. The cipher only yields a proximate not an exact dialogue for us, but it is very close to the actual meanings. The content unpacked in this verbal exchange between the "woman" and the "serpent" exposes a discussion between the woman, the serpent, and some additional women who were present. Moreover, the immediate topics—both primeval and modern day in substance—focused on *rage* in persons (concerned psychology) and *wages* to be paid (concerned financing), perhaps to the participating women, modes of anger, how to pay people, and how to make money, including earnings. It is mentioned that most women in the academy (Hall) did not oppose cunnilingus. God thought ahead all women! Women he (the serpent) thinks to enter to aid women down in area (vagina). We (women) *mad* [defeat/defile a man] had God down low. We (women) thought choose "head" works as field of study led by fine women. He (man) thinks fond of *stuff* [female finds you straight or stupid/ fist full you take sin]. Then all the people that were present were asked to enter a random thought. Thought offered: Lips I tip (head of penis) be sin. We open-mindedly saw a serpent. He thinks, no way! The dialogue continues with the statements: Enter rage thought, thinks found out wee-wee are tricked. We thought *found* "out" *fruit* [**"it" you** (our opposition) **ours** (our own would remain) **fine** (that is, unharmed)]. He thinks find out by eating women all meant we worked together to achieve a common goal, we women have power. Serpent we thought to entice you, said the woman. He (serpent) thinks cunnilingus. As the interaction continues, we get: We marry. We women first find you straight or stupid. "It" *touch* [choice out] I. We why Hall is *neither* [her it we end] it. Found out eat not favored by the Hall. We women said thoughts: Sin . . . in I sane taught head game you to hate/heat. A mind somehow opened to public [secular?] scrutiny. A "head" God. Enter rage thought. Found out stuff done I (man) mind. He (man) thinks sin I (myself) chose. I (serpent) "head" (semen) ways wee-wee are tricked into having his thoughts opened. We thoughts fond of *fruit* (results). We thought find out *time(s) you* (serpent) coitus woman. I found that these immediate comments are presented as an admixture of direct statements and otherwise as thoughts and discussions alluded to.

Gen 3:14–15: God talking to the serpent

QUOTE

And the Lord God said unto the serpent, because thou hast done this, thou art cursed above all cattle, and above every beast of the field; upon thy belly shalt thou go, and dust shalt thou eat all the days of thy life: And I will put enmity between thee and the woman, and between thy seed and her seed; it shall bruise thy head, and thou shalt bruise his heel.

<u>Interpretation</u>

I had initially thought to separate the interpretations of what are two distinct ciphers of the conversation between God and the serpent. However, I decided not to because they represent an excellent example of how thoughts can be compressed. And I am focused on content and not form and on summary meanings. In this case, the thoughts are compressed as a method of concealing insidious activity. As it turns out, the matter before us is far more complicated and intriguing than I first imagined. First God admits to the serpent that he caught him (God) in a lie. The serpent said to God, "You lied," and God admitted that he had lied to the serpent. However, God did not mean a "lie" in the conventional sense of the term. God meant that things were done as he had purposed them to be done. The serpent meant that because God had created the woman and she had "lied" to the serpent; then God necessarily "created" the lie, being in collusion with the woman and that the woman's true thoughts were not actually found out. Her thought was the thought that God put inside of her. The thought to acquire the ability or activate the ability to know the thoughts of the man. To accomplish this, she would enlist the aid of the serpent, conveniently placed. The scenario was based on a deceitful use of natural sexual attraction, where the wee-wee was juxtaposed to the Priapus to divert thought and attention away from its *insidious* purpose. Mind you, we are still within the context of thought and the learning of critical thinking, while proposing a means for women to exploit the "thought" processes of a man. It is akin to the concept of using other people's money to advance one's own personal interests; by design, it is the stratagem of opportunistically using the available thoughts of other anonymous thinkers rather than doing the hard work of critically thinking for oneself. Sexual perversion is the catalyst here. The ingestion of the combined semen of the woman and the serpent "opened" the head of the man to be exploited. Somehow after that she was able to read the man's thoughts. To call the behavior—cunnilingus—a sin seems an understatement and a diversion away from its real result and consequences. The serpent thought it was his way of demeaning the man. The woman knew it was her way of *defeating and defiling* the man and having power over him. And God purposed this behavior to help man learn how to think and understand the difference between good and evil. However, once discovered the laity (larger viewing audience) viewed it as a *fatal* flaw in a man and initially acted accordingly. The narrative alludes to why so few victims of the technique were found above ground, or by the time they were found the *"bad odor—of* their decaying bodies had—*already cursed the art."* Because when you think about an internal entity spying on one's own thoughts, it is a potential threat to privacy and public security depending on the victim's given status in the larger group or society, on the negative side. On the other hand, as monitored in the unknowing subject it is or reflects the *zeitgeist* of an *era*, over the span of an individual's lifetime—another way of saying "the breath of life" of garnered personal wisdom and knowledge. All penned as clandestinely recorded revelations. The narrative also suggests that the victim who senses what has been done to them will come to rage, madness, and to hate the life ahead of them knowing that some entity within them is "present" with them knowing their every inner thought. Thus, creating an incentive to suicide as a by-product.

To women it's a way of living their intellectual and practical lives, vicariously, yet in emotional and financial solvency, given the obvious ancillary mechanisms that can be creatively attached to her behavior for monetization. Enjoying the spoils of what amounts to a war on for the control of men, granted and revealed to her by God. The ramifications and by-products of these events being revelations on the content as the prime mover of critical thought. In the interim, the unwitting wee-wee would simply be thinking it—cunnilingus—is nothing more than a means of bringing a woman to sexual arousal and orgasm for heightened pleasure and easier vaginal penetration. The narrative states that the wee-wee is typically too busy down in the area with lascivious thirst to even consider an alternative scenario to a pleasure motive. Whereas the sight alone of the Priapus would naturally bring the woman immediately to heat (arousal), not hate. The well-spring of her hate is probably having to perform fellatio "first," thereby aiding the deception while legitimately encouraging his, the males, reciprocity. Lastly, it should be clear that the serpent was the first to impregnate the woman. Initiating the idea that there would be trouble between the serpent's seed and her seed, between Cain (the serpent's seed) and Abel (Adam's seed).

Gen. 4: 6–15: God talking with Cain.

QUOTE

And the Lord said unto Cain, why art thou wroth? And why is thy countenance fallen? If thou doest well, shalt thou not be accepted? And if thou doest not well, sin lieth at the door. And unto thee shall be his desire, and thou shalt rule over him. And Cain talked with Abel his brother: and it came to pass, when they were in the field, that Cain rose up against Abel his brother, and slew him. And the Lord said unto Cain, where is Abel thy brother? And he said, I know not: Am I my brother's keeper? And he said, what hast thou done? the voice of thy brother's blood crieth unto me from the ground. And now art thou cursed from the earth, which hath opened her mouth to receive thy brother's blood from "her hand" (the part the woman played in it all together with the serpent). When thou tillest the ground, it shall not henceforth yield unto thee her strength; a fugitive and a vagabond shalt thou be in the earth. And Cain said to the Lord, my punishment is greater than I can bear. Behold, thou hast driven me out this day from the face of the "earth" (Cain's wife); and from thy face shall I be hid; and I shall be a fugitive and a vagabond in the earth; and it shall come to pass, that every one that findeth me shall slay me. And the Lord said unto him, therefore whosoever slayeth Cain, vengeance shall be taken on him sevenfold, And the Lord set a mark upon Cain, lest any finding him shall kill him.

Earlier I gave an example of how compressed the cipher can be. At this point, let me illustrate just how raw a cipher can be, even though I am using my key in a circuitous way and not in its most specific detail. Exercised for my own clarification, I will first cipher the quote as four separate paragraphs and then as a combined cipher while limiting the specific range of my key's exposure. Consequently, I understand that my approach forces the reader to have to endure several unclear passages that follow but be confident that they will be followed by informed explanations. To wit, these two comparative approaches will be followed by my interpretation, but first, let me bullet some of the highlights of the ciphered discussions (which span both primeval and contemporary content outcomes) as findings:

- Academia is a "lay" arena in "we" mind.
- Marriage is an afterthought in "we" mind.
- The action "It" is frequent under the Hall's authority.
- Academia is a "fag" domain.

- Hall (academia) hides their real face.
- Women indict is how "we" found out.
- Modem academia's politics and policies.
- Relation of women to academia.
- Higher morality, acceptance-rejection by inner circles.
- Homosexuality.
- Lies.
- Relations of Cain with Abel in their time.

FIRST CIPHER

Me lays Hall scene, me the find. After thoughts one woman view, we. After thought pass to come Hall sit down in area. That hour already wee-wees hint bond a game already found/find. Already done in area fugitive already be. Already head is done/down in area. Hid be I sin already head-face (fellatio-cunnilingus). Why/white/women thoughts *form* [mind for] down in area. He-art he thinks found/find out face. We thoughts *form* why already done. His time out me driven. Stuff ahead you hot/to hate. Hold be is ear can I enter already thought greater. Are time men punishing, women mind own do/did/done.

He thinks to enter you aids Cain [end I all see]. Down in area woman we hint "be you" to hate. Halt sin. Bond a game all found. All down in area fugitive. A strength her wee-wee taught to end you yield thought for. Hence touch [choose out] on Hall sit wound game. He thinks illest time you open thought in the ways. Hand women thought from blood (menstruation). Bothers our woman thought receive to mouth. Her opened thought ahead choose I hear ways. Her we thoughts form cursed you out.

Thought's art now! Down in area wound game. He thinks mind for me to enter you. He thinks I hours see blood (menstruation) brother's woman. Thoughts found open voice. He thinks done you

78

hot(aroused). Stuff ahead after had words. Said he did/done in area. Hours he keeps brother's woman. Mind I am! Not know I said he did in area. Brother woman thought Abel is where Cain to enter you did/done. *Him* [mine/mind I head] *way we lick seen / way we liked scene / we looked seen* done in area.

Brother [other ours be] his Abel stuff put you, we it our Cain. After thought did lie, we found hint: **were they?** [why he thinks we *are* we ways?!] (Resulted in their being the approbate [after a probe . . . proof].) Entered he way. Ass-penis to me, all see "it" done in area. (*They committed homosexual acts between* **themselves**.) Brother is head. Abel head-wit Cain down into area. I am head few overrule. Halt sin *you* to hate. Down in the area desire is head! *We* be all shush, wee-wee thought to enter you down in area. **Door/odor (remember, a door can serve as both an entrance and an exit).** He thinks after thought—Lie! Enter is low lips way, not stuff *we* do. You hate, if down in area accepted. *We* be not you! Hot, halt sin! Well stuff *we* did. You to hate *found* [did end *you* . . . out *first* (time sin hour I find)] I. (Cain and Abel were obviously communicating telepathically here, because Cain is threatening Abel with what he will do to him once he finds him.)

SECOND and Combined CIPHER

We mind lay hall sense. We mind thoughts we find after thoughts, one woman. A few we after thoughts pass to me over sees Hall's "it" done in area. Heart, he thinks we hint bond. Already fag, already down in area. We I fit game you found already. We be Hall's I done in area. Hid be I Hall's face because thoughts form down in area. Heart, he thinks found out face we thoughts from women indict. His time me driven out. Time has you hot. Hold we be ear; be can I enter ahead time we great, since I time men punish women mind. Down low he thinks to aid sin already sees done in area. Heart, we hint we be you hot. Halt since, bond a fag. Already down in area fugitive. Already strength her wee-wee thoughts to enter you yield forth we see, end. The (we thought) no Hall sit. Wound game he thinks **lest** look it you hot. When hand her form do opens like be some other, ours be thoughts receive to mouth. Her opened thoughts ahead which earth he thinks form did. Some cure you hot art now. Done ends area wound game. He thinks form to enter you cried blood others bar. Why? Thought found out voice. We thought done. You hot straight ahead what said he down in area. Hours we keep others bar. Women mind I am. Time is not now kept; I aid him down in area. Her time rob women head time. Able since I where enter I all see to enter. Your "ad" is down low we head time did end already. He slew down in area. Her to bar: His able straight again. Pussy you rose in I all see _that_ [after thought] time. Led I found we hint we are we women, the hen way. After passing to my _cat_ [after sees], I down in area. Brother is here able head wit. Do we tell in all seen done in area? His overrule halt us hot down in area. Desire his be looks like has wee-wee thoughts to end you down in area, _door_ [odor/ours often do]. We thought that lie. Sin well time no time does. You hot if do enter area accepted. Bet no, you hot halts well. Time does you hot found I. Fallen we can we count. Why this woman hand way thoughts wow. You hot women _head wart_ I can. To enter you _said_ . . . _and the_ [we (we way) thoughts done, ended already] / [death ended] (Education's end thoughts we already did.).

Interpretation
(Gen. 4:6–24)

Having ciphered this discussion between God and Cain regarding the act that he "slew" his brother, let us first review what the Scripture tells us led up to the "act." Apparently, Cain was the first to bring his offering to God then Abel followed. God accepted Abel's offering and rejected Cain's. So Cain became very distraught [aught hours' time seen I did (stand for something)]. Clearly Cain had put in more physical labor than Abel having worked an already cursed ground surface to yield edible food. But God made Cain aware of what he knew about the two brothers' actual relationship by hinting that there must have been some sin {"sin lieth at the door" (odor) . . . Gen. 4:7} involved that effected God's evaluation overall. And God suggests to Cain that he is aware of what will happen between he and Abel. For God said: "And unto thee *shall be* his desire, and thou shall rule over him" (Gen. 4:7). The original text implies that Cain slew Abel out of jealousy or resentment concerning God's better favor. However, God hints of a *back story* that the cipher reveals, and more. I initially separated this cipher into four consecutive paragraphs and what is revealed is threaded across an ancient story. However, when the text is combined and ciphered, I discovered within its findings a relation to a contemporary scenario; thus, affirming God's knowledge of all that happens even before it happens and reasserts the reality of God's "double speak."

Paragraph *one* speaks to the more contemporary idea that most families want their kin to stay close to the nest, and abide by their traditional moral and social precepts, so monitored for their own well-being. For example, one finds a locally familiar person to *marry* for life. Thus families "lay" the idea of running off to college and being exposed to multiple potential sexual partners, for religious or spiritual reasons. (This speaks to the pervasively conservative nature of family structure and thus the kernel of modern societal outlook.) They warn or hint that "bonding" at college is a legal game that has real consequences for their future. Which is not qualitatively different from the consequences in the local neighborhood but in a way that is formally hidden and unspoken. You become a "fugitive" from home and local society, once you have had experience enough to uncover/discover the prohibition that *dominant* society at large places on moral conduct and behavior. Behavior primarily based on whether you have engaged sexually in fellatio or cunnilingus. Seemingly trivial and innocent, this is major and serious stuff. You silently become a *pariah* [head already . . . I our "A" personality]. In intimate ways you become *ostracized* [did we scheme?

I see already our stuff out] by family and rejected by the academy. In ancient times, it was considered a "banishment." In modem times, to seek a doctorate or PhD is to ask the academy for the opportunity to have access to sacred higher learning or the "greater thought." It speaks to one's *desire* to be *"verb intransitive"* [found I we sit . . . want in . . . I be few/view] (my emphasis). In full acknowledgement of what already is the contrasted *dilemma* [*meal-minded . . . I do (wedding vows)*]. Therefore in the contemporary version of the revelations, we have families wanting to keep their kin connected to family matters, influences, and local community; and concurrently, we have the fallacy of the innocence of the college as one's private/definite dream fulfilling experience, the *setup* where not only your ability but your *moral behavior* is being scrutinized and unwittingly tested, pass/fail. What appears the lesser political challenge, and certainly the least problematic, is the master's degree. I find it ironic that most of the wealthiest people on the planet *do not have a college degree*, yet some of the poorest people on the planet *do have* college degrees.

[*paragraph 2*] Abel approached Cain's (Yes!) wife to have sex with her under the pretense of bonding to help Cain out. A game or ruse apparently played in those days. What Abel did not know was that Cain had taught his wife ("a strength") that the person that would perform cunnilingus on her would eventually come to *hate* her, and not desire her anymore. It was a strategy to halt the sin of adultery. Any male performing cunnilingus was thus considered a "fugitive." Her tactic to avoid having intercourse with Abel was to offer him fellatio and cunnilingus only, which potentially contained Cain's live semen, in lieu of intercourse. Performing those acts would also technically and legally exclude Abel from qualifying to have formally approved and privileged access to levels of "greater thought" at the academy. Her effort was a "wound game." Abel's initial thought was simply that the "illest" time to perform cunnilingus was when a woman was on her "period." In fact, the occurrence of a woman's menstruation cycle was one reason men began rejecting oral sex and resorted to using their hands to arouse a woman to the point of orgasm or intercourse. At that same time—simultaneous to—Cain's wife was *"thinking"* cunnilingus, Abel's wife *"thought"* "receive to mouth." Her thought in tandem with Cain's wife's thought was a stand-in for, Abel's wife **to have "cursed out"** Abel. Here we get a hint of the notion that human thought is connected, has formally been connected, and can be connected. What is implied in the cipher is that God and consequently mankind were *preoccupied with the dynamics of thought*—for its own sake—in that day. Moreover, it appears that some chosen of mankind have been given the unique power or skill to read the thoughts of each other; and even in effect to alter the thoughts of others. With which, by way of intense concentrative skill, some had greater ability in this regard than others. Specifically, it would turn out that Abel's "thought skills" or powers were much stronger than Cain's.

[*paragraph 3*] Paragraph 3 begins with the writer's narrative suggesting that what immediately follows is somewhat sketchy, because he deliberately makes an ambiguous statement. We are left to determine which does he mean: The way out ended time, as in death, like the people who were observing thought, or does he mean "thought" had advanced so much by that time man could read minds and actual control, in real time, the minds of other men?! Thus "thought" would have become an *"art form."* Or did he mean both? Then we are suddenly given more clarity. Abel says to Cain's wife to admit that you just used a "wound game" on me. That statement is followed by the comment "done," in reply to Abel. Abel then begins using his thought power to program the woman's mind to desire to have intercourse with him. He thinks a "desire" to have his "blood" brother's woman for hours. Thereafter, he thought open your vagina, and the two of them saw "it open." That is, her desire for Abel became so intense that the two of them literally watched her vagina open. He then thinks done, she is "hot" ["to hate" . . . or reached the point of arousal, if you will], and *stuff* went ahead

83

after they had words. The text reveals that what Abel said he did, he did in the area (of her vagina) for hours. The text says for hours he "wee-wee" kin brother's woman. Then after having taken control and having his way with her he boosted "Mind I Am," emphasizing his exceptional mind-control ability. Cain then says to God, "I did not know he entered her vagina . . . that they reached coitus." God informs Cain that, through the women's thoughts and the actual scenes, he is aware that Cain had performed *similar* acts with Abel's wife. Cain said "we" (he and God) looked (through an apparently special mechanism of thought) and saw the scene God had in mind, by some apparently supernatural visualization process. The text suggests that Cain and Abel may have been with each other's wives simultaneously. In fact, the writer of the text did mean "sketchy." Some details are missing that could have filled out the story. Perhaps paragraph 4 will help ***illuminate*** [eat entered I mind . . . your lips liked I /eat in mind . . . you ill] the details.

[*paragraph 4*] As the narrative continues, we get: additional hours of Cain-Abel *stuff* He ***"took you put you"*** meaning Abel performed anal sex on Cain and had Cain also perform oral sex on him. Of course, they had both committed adultery with each other's wives. So the text suggests the wrongs they did to each caused the scales to appear to be balanced, to a point. The balancing was apparently based on which acts were performed and by whom on the part of each of the four persons, with cunnilingus and fellatio promulgating "hate." However, upon further thought and reflection, something did not add up. Because the *monitors/observers* had to "it" (sanction) Cain (meaning Cain acted in a way sexually that de facto gave him cause to hate) in the balancing despite the fact (attempting to follow the logic) he had not performed cunnilingus either on his own or Abel's wife. Concentrated thought upon directed reflection found the "lie" ["we" I lip]. A hint was found by the monitors. Even though Cain and Abel may have attempted to disguise their mental thought content, the investigators picked up on what they tried to hide mentally. The hint was ***"were they?!"*** [Hey there, we are we ways]. The hint was the result of their being induced through *thought __approbate__* [after a probe . . . proof]. That is, the result was obtained after their "thoughts" were *somehow* legally investigated. The commission's finding was that the sin which generated an *imbalance* in the sins committed between Cain and Abel was the result of their *homosexual relations*. Cain had performed fellatio on Abel, but it was **not** reciprocated. By way of cipher, the text reveals the first hour was anal sodomy and the other hour was fellatio. Abel's mind *witted* Cain down into the area. Abel then exclaimed, "I am head few overrule . . . Halt sin, **you** hate!" said Abel. Abel's meaning here is that *opposition to sin* is what is to be hated, not sin itself. (It is instructive to understand the *point* is that Cain was against the sin of oral sex, specifically cunnilingus, and wished to end it.) "Down in area **desire** is head," said Abel. He goes on to say: "'We' be . . . shush thought (blot it out from your mind) wee-wees to have entered (you Cain) down in area." This suggests a feeble attempt on Abel's part to try and thwart the potential outcome in the probe of their thoughts. The text then simply says, The **door (odor).** What minimally is the door of opportunity for Cain to escape and exit the mess, the afterthought, *Lie.* Entering the mess is "low lips ways" (fellatio or cunnilingus). Cain says, "'It' was not stuff 'we' do." Cain did something sinful that Abel did not do (fellatio on Abel). Thus, the lie! Once he figured it out, Cain said to Abel, "You to hate, if fellatio is not accepted. 'We' be not 'you'!" (In other words, you have not played fair, Abel.) To hate halts sin (the sin of adultery) was the "well" stuff we did (they each performed cunnilingus on the other's wife), says Cain. (This last statement helps to highlight the imbalance in the sins committed by the two brothers; because *it makes clear* that while Cain *did not* do cunnilingus with his own wife, *he did* do cunnilingus and likely coitus with Abel's wife.) Once the established imbalance was acknowledged. Cain said to Abel, "You *are* the one to be hated and you are found!" Therefore, Cain's [same end I all see (*it*-targeted I)] hate *slew* (way we liked scene) Abel (*that*-afterthought). Hence, Abel was the first to be recorded to have been *slain* [end I all slick/end I all licks sin] on earth, if you will.

This may all seem and sound a "mess" until we remind ourselves that God is involved (God may have rested on the seventh day of creation but his work obviously did not end there) and God is *still* actively participating in helping man to learn how to think. *Sin* is the catalyst for moving "thought" forward. However, we cannot now know for sure whether these are actual events or a <u>*simulation*</u> [entered openly I (God) talk. Always you listen. Mind senses I/No, after licking you, matters I sense/ in open I target all like you means I sin], because they are thoughts revealed in a cryptographic medium. And the whole intent and focus was on thought and thinking, that was *the context of reality in action back then* as I find it recorded in the proffered scriptural text. However, the meanings are clear. Learning about the differences between right and wrong behavior a.k.a. good and evil, as an active continuum of learning and emotional growth through personal or vicarious experience. Thus, in the immediate scenarios, we are introduced to a view of sinning as a balancing act: a tit-for-tat or blow-for-blow conscious activity, was what the characters in the action thought was the correct thing to do. It was kind of a nod to the false notion of "an eye for an eye, tooth for a tooth." However, Cain found the way out of that structure by discovering the concept of and applying the concept of "hate." Thus *sin* [internally I have seen] not only *exists—with cunnilingus appearing the more abhorrent—but* it is also a metaphor for finding oneself. For finding the "we" in the "I" of self. Shortly, I will explain the meaning of the "we" in "I" phraseology noted here. In the interim, I wish to explain the concepts that issue from Cain's two spirited comments in his explicit replies to God. I need to unpack this so that you understand why God was able to change his mind about Cain's destiny.

The cipher reveals that in Cain's reply to God's query—about the whereabouts of his brother Abel: "I know not. Am I my brother's keeper"—there are several informative threads of meaning to be uncovered. The first one is: God are you not the God who said my brother you would keep?! Cain was expressing *sarcasm and indignation* [nation get ideas in . . . down in area always scars] here. A second thread of meaning is: *Hours we keep sin her told openly rob woman's* [*man's over weighted*] *mind. I am saying No to cunnilingus/fellatio. Now okay I.* Third, yet another more expanded meaning relates: Since hour you (God) opened our heads "we" kept sin. (Let us be clear, within these contexts, the word *sin* [inside I sane / internally I seen/ Sin (female)] has these multiple meanings.) Her I met; time you opened our heads we have agreed. But the woman's head was weighted down in being *"mad"* [**defeated** (Did we eat first? We did!) **a man** / **defiled a man** (man already lied fine we did)]. *I (Cain) also became depressed* until I (Cain) *mad* [defeated a "mind" / a thought (referencing Abel's demise)]. I down inside I mind looked like all I met out ended. Woman a way out entered I . . . okay ended another I . . . (Abel). A fourth and final expansion goes as follows: Since hour you (God) opened our heads we kept "Sin." Her (Sin) I met time you opened our heads. Wee-wee woman be head weighted down in "I mad." I mind looked like all I met told you (Cain) to keep God out of it. Defeated we *ended* women always tell you (God) out. The deed ended okay I.

The meanings here are consistent. Oral sex by then had become a major sociopolitical issue, as a "sin" and a social problem. Yet the option was opened for the individual to choose the correct behavior. The tension here is over Cain's struggle to define and defend the correct sexual behavior between male and female. Thus, the implication that a woman who is *aware* and really *cares* about a man will discourage him from performing or desiring to perform cunnilingus with her. If, on the other hand, he insists she will come to hate him, and be willing to indict him revealing his conduct to others to be sanctioned socially. Bottom line, men commonly will "desire" to perform oral sex on a woman, because they believe it will almost certainly open her mind and body to a willingness to allow him intercourse with her, especially if he has a very small penis, and not a Priapus. But it goes deeper than that. In her mind a man is "defeated" once he performs cunnilingus, because it potentially subjects him unwittingly to a form of homosexuality, either as a target, "it," or as an afterthought, "that." The *"alternative to that* or *it"* (a.k.a. "instead thereof" Gen. 2:21) is men not engaging in oral sex at all, period [down out . . . I phew/pew].

Remember, "God caused a deep sleep to fall upon Adam" (Gen. 2:21) [To paraphrase: **mad already ended opening sexual play. You already found out ink's thoughts. Women someone sent you a Priapus . . . representing a woman's overwhelming "desire" for a large penis. Wee-wee lips same Sin. Dad use all see.**] (More literally: **defiled a man already . . . No! People you all find out times Priapus, wee-wee licks seed. Priapus, wee-wee dad use already sees do game.**) Yes. God's ***words*** are sharper than two-edged ***words (my emphasis)***.

After Cain slew Abel, God said to Cain, *"And now art thou cursed from the earth which has opened her mouth to receive thy brother's blood from thy hand"* (Gen. 4:11). He goes on to tell Cain that nothing productive will come from his labor and he would be a fugitive and a vagabond. These were very strong words. He banished Cain from the earth, in a word, yet changed his mind and put a "mark" of protection from danger from others on Cain. The following statement by Cain changed God's mind: ***"My punishment is greater than I can bear. Behold, thou hast driven me out this day from the face of the earth; And from thy face shall I be hid; And I shall be a fugitive and a vagabond in the earth; and it shall come to pass, that every one that findeth me shall slay me"*** *(Gen. 4:13–14).* I wanted to get some idea of what he said in that explicit reply. First, God's curse translates as, "Down in ahead woman thought . . . Cain *got away* from do outlook . . . be sin brother. Why she thought receive to 'mouth' [thoughts you out mind (Abel)]. She did open encounter as 'head' choice. For I will heal given the way thought will air. He inks form (woman) did *curse you* on (Abel's) head. That 'wart' (*condyloma* [already mind outlook women do end . . . *out see*]) *down in area."*

Now we can see Cain's response to what God spoke was **"thought negotiations"** [thought sin out after I got (understood) "we" internally]. For the first sentence of Cain's response translates as: "God listen. Be 'we' for a moment. Enter I (my mind) all see 'I' ended all bad thoughts my wee-wee had—after learning about 'we'—have changed to **good** (*as in good versus evil*). Since that time, I have been telling men about 'head,' oral sex, sin. I enter you (God) *'perfect'* [time . . . see we find our 'we' partners] . . . (help me find—a virtuous—woman/women who do not and will not insist that men commit the cardinal sin . . . cunnilingus . . . and be able to receive from their women open, honest, and committed natural affection). *'Women' [men outweighed] 'mind'* [done in I *mad* (defiled a man)/ *'desire'* [we are I sin we do]." *(It took a man's mind to defeat a man's mind and to end the cycle.)* In other words, Cain acknowledges his sin and professes he is changed and has been working to change others by informing them of what his sins were.

Additionally, when I cipher Cain's quote, I get the following content (which by the way also introduces a contemporary context): We mind lays sin. Hall's (the academy's) sin we *mind* the found after thoughts. One's very "eats" thought ass people to come. Hall's sit down ends already our thoughts ear. We hint bond already *fag* and already fugitive A ("A" represents a person who seeks formal education. Someone who has the audacity to want, by way of formal education, to make something of themselves.). To be Hall's is to be done in already, hide **"be I"** Hall's sin "face"! Women thoughts *form* down in area. Thoughts ear (air) he thinks. We thoughts found out *face*. We thoughts from women DA (indict) his time, out me driven. Straight ahead you hot/rage. Old head (God) we be (we ask) bear (tolerate us) getting rid of this form of "me." Enter (intervene to thwart bad behavior) ahead (conviction) time; *greater(better)* <u>*since*</u> [we see sin]. I time men <u>*punish*</u> [shush I in you put] women mind.

The gist of these comments is clear. In addition to Cain asking God to help him find a virtuous woman, he is also asking God not to object to his efforts to eliminate the sin of cunnilingus as relates to men. He is also asking God to explain how he gives women the ability to read men's minds. He is asking, how does it work? These comments also speak to women's doublemindedness on this matter and the Hall's laissez-faire attitude on these pertinent matters. The bottom line is that, in thought and action, Cain repented to God for his earlier behavior. As a result, God apparently forgave him for every wrong he had done.

As to Cain's legacy, the Scripture records that he went on to build *a city* (Gen. 4:17). Therefore, God did not in the end condemn Cain to being a fugitive and vagabond. On the contrary and in addition, Cain went on to father three sons, and through his sons and their progeny the mastery of the fields of music, metallurgy, and husbandry were founded and established for mankind. In other words, Cain was not just forgiven, he was both protected and rewarded, he received God's favor! (Gen. 4:15–22).

Gen. 2:25: Concerning man and his wife's nakedness

QUOTE

And they were both naked, the man and his wife, and were not ashamed.

Do You Want To Hear About It?

FIRST CIPHER

[med (educated mate) ahead as time {I met} No, down in area. We if way is head down in area man, we thoughts education kept "nah" to be we are we . . . why he thinks {inks thoughts} down in area.]

SECOND CIPHER

We mad. (Made way/ ad mind we weighed) has time. On (brain opened) we are . . . we weighs/ ways down in area. Wife, his own down in area! Man, he *thinks* [inks thoughts] **done we kept all in!** Thought out . . . **Brew** (transfer of what equates to a germ—simultaneous admixture of live male and female semen—internally to a *male* orally) eye thoughts done ended "A" (personality).

THIRD CIPHER

Did shame before No! We are we ways down in area. Wife is head done in area; man, he thinks don't we kept . . . already into thoughts out. Brew we way women her times—*dues* [sue did/ sue ideas done] in area.

FOURTH CIPHER

Education we "sham" before No. We are we done in area. We if way is his down in area. Man, he thinks education kept in ahead time. Out he wee-wees' Hey there down in area. Or Man he thinks naked thoughts opened be our women eye (see) thoughts down in always.

Interpretation

An ominous reality is being acknowledged or exposed here also. There is a clear and unequivocal indication that one's thoughts are *magically* opened to public scrutiny by others once being submitted to oral sex. One's thoughts are read—involuntarily. This capability apparently absolutely exists. What is repeated here and was strongly suggested earlier is that oral sex is considered such a "moral" taboo in greater dominant society, for the above reason and more that it **"opens a window** into a person's mind," either as something to ridicule people about or to seriously be concerned about because of *"it" engendering real psychosomatic illness* [senses seen we entered ill. See I after minds opened. Sensed opened head . . . see why people look around. Around we are! Ring {*the* **bell:** *live like we believe he thinks} we ended gotten into . . . we "it"*]—; and oral sex behavior is potentially *advertised—as in an ad—in* the media; even when discovered happening between consenting spouses. Moreover, the text appears to suggest that a woman performing fellatio on a man, does not possess the strict moral turpitude as does a male performing cunnilingus, given the revelations regarding homosexuality.

With respect to the serpent versus "other beasts of the field" (Gen. 3:1) [Deciding life "we" if we thoughts found out sin stuff [first found out you stupid] already we be . . . her time out "opening" [game into I pen out]! That is, so others of the men present on the planet are/ were able to learn many critical things about life *vicariously*—not by direct experience but—by *observation and study of the defiant behavior of others and their actual thoughts.*

I proffered these notes as the ***gist*** of the concept of the *"afterthought"* began to ***emerge*** or take form in my mind. I was about to begin my explanation of the concept of "we," when I got side-tracked by the following: and, as it turns out, very instructive scriptural quotation: *"God is a spirit; and they that worship him must worship him in spirit and in truth"* (John 4:24). In that moment, my spirit had directed me to the ***concept*** that ***crystallizes*** [size tall *soon* women are see] what I have been attempting to better understand and explain when discussing the

92

"unpacking" of a statement. It is first the "thought" then the "afterthought." First the *manifest* content and then the *latent* content. The afterthought *images* the thought. Thus, the above quoted Scriptural statement in John. 4:24—first as the *thought*—yields the *afterthought*: [Truth {thoughts you are taught} . . . entering I down in area. Wit I perfect. Sin, I am head, hips, wow stuff you meant. I am "here" hips way . . . our ways after thought. *Why?* {women head ways} he touches down in area. Wit I perfect, as is *God.*] As an afterthought here, I am reminded of the "subtil" nature attributed to the serpent. When in fact what was *"subtle"* about the sexual encounters the woman had with the serpent is she used his Priapus for her own immediate pleasure and satisfaction. **She was enthralled with the serpent's Priapus (organ) not with his mind (person).** She then influenced his thoughts to assist her in tricking Adam. *The subtlety was in the woman making lustful sex to the serpent's Priapus specifically and then using his mind, to help her carry out God's plan.* Remember God admitted that he deceived the serpent in believing the serpent's own thought influenced the woman to trick Adam. It should be clear from these comments that the woman initially exerted a powerful and definitive influence along with God in these matters.

Another content rich example of *thought* and *afterthought* results from the statement, **thought:** "No *weapon that is formed against thee shall prosper; and every tongue that shall rise against thee in judgement thou shalt condemn."* **Afterthought:** [Entering me done. No, seen! Halt sin you to hate times men judge in wee-wee thoughts street again. Wise Halls afterthought tongue women few we down in area prosper [pews pro]. Hall's wee-wee thoughts against educate from, since I that {afterthought}no power already, we *way* (even more so) no.] Doubtless, this last afterthought explains itself.

Thus **Thought:** *"In the beginning God created the heaven (male) and the earth (female). And the earth was without form [mind for] and* *void [ideas out front]; and darkness [seen sized/seized we entered dark] was upon the face of the deep. And the spirit of God moved upon the face of the waters*" (Gen. 1:1–2). And now the **Afterthought:** [Waste hours we thought found out . . . face, he thinks on people you do. We found out mind do games. Fine offer . . . *with* (head with) . . . sip. He inks thoughts: Own out did . . . entered I all we are after. People wee-wee did, he inks thought, found out "face." He inks thought on people you were seen, since we ended dark. Own out do in areas idea out. Found own out! Own out done in area formed out head. With as way, *thoughts ear* [are already we] *(female). He* thinks down in area thoughts female. We thought down in area into we find him. He thinks do we eat ours? See did *go* game in I end? Begin! He thinks entered I.]

Thought [taught head game you to hate] = *Adam* [mad already] = *male/female* [we look around men fee . . . left around money] = *heaven/ earth* [thoughts are . . . even around he] = *them* [men we have taught].

Hence **Thought:** "*And breathed into his nostrils the breath of life; and man became a living soul*" (Gen. 2:7). And then the **Afterthought:** "[Lips you (serpent) 'opened' sin. Game in I fine / found I like lips. After me already see. We be man down in area . . . life (lie found) / evil found out. Head eat be her *stuff* {first find you stupid}. Lips I are straight, No! Sense I head to enter I door/odor, we **hand** eat ours. We (we ways) be done in area.] This is why the serpent called the woman (or 'help meet') Sin."

The **Thought:** "Help meet" (Gen. 2:20). **Afterthought:** [[took wee-wee "mind"?! . . . Pussy! [why (women head ways) since seen you penis] lips [seen pussy I like] . . . we head.]] This was prophetic!

Thought: *Escape ability to be provoked.* **Afterthought:** [Did we okay offer. Found out ours/hours already sees sin we [we weighs / we ways / we wage].

My Thoughts: *After considering the facts I am developing; I am convinced that a man child's (males) life is in part socially constructed, in thought, by his immediate significant others. And is based on his assessed sexual **potential** [life after I Potent] . . . determined by his mother's judgement, concerning the size of his penis . . . weewee or Priapus. "Thought" toward him concentrates on his penis size.* **Afterthought:** We scheme is senses I pen. His No! Sum, rate, cent no sees. Mind I have seen toward "thought." Sin you thought Priapus or wee-wee. Penis his fine/find *over* size. We thought got in I concern time [me it] men we game. Do your job, since the other mind is head. Women be do mind deter [potent I after lie found]. *Potential* [look already I potent.]. Sexual did we assess?! Sense I heard . . . No! Did we sign already *bet is* . . . done entering already others can tell if I sign ate idea. Me aim his by thought in me. Did we construct ally [women live life already?!] I see opening such is life, senses man child already afterthought. Did convince mind already I am developing. Mind already I fact, senses he thinks considering after {our we time found already}.

The points being made here are that our personal thoughts inform our behavior, thought is spirit based; and spirit is ultimately a connected sociocultural spiritual construct. A construct wherein not only our own personal thoughts but the thoughts of others arbitrarily imposed on us influence our actions. Thoughts *as data* come from outside us and intermingle as created thought with the spirit within us. In other words, our lives are circumscribed by what amounts to a concentration camp type concept of focused oversight, based specifically on our actual, perceived, and potential *sexually based* behavioral outlook and experiences. Where sexual behavior informs lifestyles; and lifestyle matters with respect to societal rewards and punishments. Thought is a social construct managed and aided by God's Holy Spirit, a very complex and difficult form of grace. Inside of each of us is an accumulated body of language and that language is a "multiplex" of ideas. That is why I believe God gave a never to be forgiven consequence to anyone who would curse the Holy spirit. The Holy spirit's delicate handywork benefiting us should account for something miraculous! (Mark 3:28–29).

First Elements

Like God, who is a spirit, man is first and foremost also a ***Spirit***. Our spirits live in a physical ***Body***, and it has a ***Soul / (Mind). The mind (a living spiritual entity) is our central nervous system controlled by the brain.*** For our purposes, we have need to concentrate most of our focus on the *mind* and the *spirit*. We must understand and accept that each of our individual spirits interacts/communicates with God as a spirit in the *mode* of spirit, whether you are aware of it, believe it, or not. That is, God speaks to us, using his Holy Spirit, through our respective spirits; and our spirits speak to our mind and our mind in turn speaks to spirit. In the interim, our mind communicates with itself. Curiously, our mind is made up of two parts. One part is ***conscious***, and the other part is ***subconscious***. The two parts communicate with each other through a process one might call *"unconscious cerebration."* In other words, the two distinct parts have discussions with each other concerning external facts and data revealed *separately* to each part by way of our central nervous system; and they then reach "tentative" conclusions about the ordering and meaning of these data without their processing being immediately awakened in our conscious thought. Thereafter, the Holy Spirit reviews the mind's findings and, through our spirit, reveals to our minds a higher clarity of timely and appropriate thought, *if we are listening*. Some call that higher clarity "intuition" [No I. Tell I, you think in I / Not I . . . it You . . . in I]. That is, when you believe, the Holy Spirit will influence the reasoning carried on between your conscious and subconscious mind, without you even being actively conscious of it. To better help you understand, with the purpose of encouraging you to embrace these concepts and start the process of listening better, let me share a real-time scenario with you.

One of the paradoxical truths about teaching is that the teacher is in a continuous state of learning by benefit of their teaching. For example, while teaching mathematics at a community college in upstate New York for some twenty-three years, I was privileged to be the recipient of a few, of what I feel are, unique pearls of wisdom. As a result of the "archetypical" fear and anxiety that students typically have toward mathematics, I *"learned"* [earned look] . . . **most people do not know how to read . . . well!** They do not read with *"discernment."* They take too many words for granted, which inhibits the learning process. For example, in elementary statistics if one cannot discern the uses and distinction between the words **"and"**; and in a different context the word, ***"or,"*** it becomes virtually impossible for that student to master the arithmetic of and concepts in *inferential* statistics. Moreover, since one is only using numbers between zero (0) and one (1) in statistics; it is essential to discern the *contextual* differences between the word *percentage, proportion, and probability* or you fail to understand the subject's *infrastructure.* Because of this lack of discernment, what is very simple will appear to be very complex. Thus, my job when teaching elementary statistics became, as is the primary pedagogical goal, *influencing* students to read with discernment, the arithmetic (addition, subtraction, multiplication, division) was the easy part.

Moreover, on one unexceptional day during class, while trying to handle the issue of "math anxiety"; and trying to convince students of the importance of reading/studying their textbooks and notes, after all they would have already paid hundreds of dollars for their textbooks, I had an epiphany: ***One cannot learn what one does not already know!*** While there are several ways to interpret this statement, what it meant at the moment has direct reference to how our brains actually work. One does not have to know any of the very technical aspects of how the brain functions to appreciate the brain's *power* and *purpose.* At every moment in time, our brain collects all immediately surrounding environmental data that it is exposed to through its five major sensory organs; and then, using what I believe ultimately is a *knowable* **cerebration** *process and yet indescribable* **spiritual** *process,* it makes sense of *the data* for conscious use. It *thinks* and has a memory function that never loses the use of the data taken in, even though we cannot calibrate it. That is, the brain forever makes use of all received data, both on the conscious and subconscious levels. Everything that the central nervous system has ever heard, seen, felt, tasted, smelled, etc., is recorded in the brain's sensory memory beginning even before we exited our mother's womb and is never lost unless the brain is physically damaged. When one begins to understand that you are not directly mentally conscious of all that your eyes, for an example, take in (see) in each day and replicate this fact times the related work of our other sensory organs; you should appreciate that it is the "subconscious" mind that is the **repository** of most of our sensory data. Therefore, it logically follows that the kernel or **core** of our understanding resides in our "subconscious" mind.

Knowing these things, I would explain to my students that if you have listened attentively to the topic discussed in each lecture and gone home reread and rewritten your notes and read what the textbook relates on the topic, given that God has given us the capacity to understand anything albeit we cannot know everything; your subconscious mind will have *already* understood the topic. The memory of what was said and then dutifully read will never be lost, at least not subconsciously, from the brain. You are left only to do the *repetitive, clarifying* work to bring the topical thoughts to the surface and into your consciously aware short-term memory. Therefore, your brain will have already retained the thought content's meanings; and thus, all that you will have to do, proactively, is **get** it, help your mind understand what it already knows. This is an illustration of how powerful your brain is in its workings. Again, one does not have to know about all the electro-chemical dynamics of neurons and sections of the brain to appreciate the brain's functional power. We can leave that knowledge to the specialists. For our purpose, knowing the above general algorithm of the brain's functioning is both necessary and sufficient.

Although I do not recall having read any major parts of his writings, I recently reviewed a recorded live interview with the famous psychologist C.G. Jung. He studied human personality and argued that it consists of the following constituent parts: **persona** (self/appearance), **Ego** (consciousness), **Mind** (subconsciousness), and **Psyche** (spirit). Ervin Goffman gives an excellent explanation and description of what amounts to Jung's *persona* element in his book *The Presentation of Self in Everyday Life*. And the very ***worthy*** sociologist C. Wright Mills further elucidates these ideas in his book *Character and Social Structure*. Here social structure simply means how primary social relationships are developed and how they come to be maintained and replicated over time.

In my own theory of understanding, the major roles are played by the conscious mind, the subconscious mind, and the psyche (Spirit). ***I believe and have come to know*** that everyone is a Spirit, that lives in a physical body, and has a soul/mind. The *mind* itself is comprised of its *conscious* and *subconscious* parts. As I mentioned earlier, the sensory organs in our body transmit usable data to these two functioning operational characteristics of the brain, which uses that data in its thinking capacity. The subconscious mind contains the larger portion of that acquired data. My Spirit communicates with the Holy Spirit and together they communicate with my mind to make sense out of God's wisdom transmitted and translated to me through spirit, to make sense of the mind's ruminations. Thus *"we think." Language being the conveyor of our thought, and the definable content of our thoughts are observable in our speech and behavior.*

Relatedly, when I began teaching myself how to cipher language, I let the letter "e," acting as one of the first elements, represent the word "me." One day while considering the nature of the conscious and subconscious mind, I realized—*my spirit revealed to me*—that my conscious mind is a unique part of **"me"** and my subconscious mind is a separate unique part of **"me,"** and since each is unique, I intuitively calculated in thought, like in addition, unique "me" plus unique "me" is equivalent to a **"we"** in me. That is, taken together they are the integral **we** of what makes up the whole I of *myself, or self.* Then, using *we* instead of *me* in every application of the letter *"e" used* subsequently, a whole new expanded world of new and usable content immediately opened to my mind. My knowledge base thus became a *plurality* rather than a *singularity.* Understanding the applications and implications of this contextual "we," **we** must be the answer to the profundity in the kinds of knowledge we all seek. This **we** become the <u>music</u> [see I sense you made] of life. The epiphany here is that this **we** in understanding is a word symbolic of a *trifecta* in categories of thought that represent the totality of the knowledge the individual or mankind will ever possess. It is we in the *"I" am* of creation: *we the words, we the ways, we the works.* Meaning, the totality of the *words* that mankind uses, the variety in the cultural *ways* of mankind, and the multiplicity of *works* that mankind has **produced**. **We** are simply that *historical* **object** we think about in general, *our created and creative thoughts.* So what we find is that from the beginning in the scriptural history of mankind, sex has been societies <u>Weltanschauung</u> [you hung? sees answers already . . . let win!]. Necessarily, it is the progenitor and prime mover of everything good and evil in the world. What amounts to our *not so uncommon* sense. Our sensual (physical) and spiritual realities are connected by God. There is no need to try and deny it. Those who pretend to deny it are consumed in either deceit or ignorance.

What I have provided for you in this treatise is simply "a notion of the notion," as Georg Wilhelm Friedrich Hegel would refer to it. Even using a theoretically and logically constructed ciphers' key, we are unable to give a perfect rendering of all the facts and intricacies to be gleaned from a scriptural yet fractured narrative as historical record.

Although language embodies these facts in toto, yet in coded form, God's Holy Spirit has allowed me and helped me to broach and bridge these matters. So we see that *"this is truly a **grown folks business** [since seen we sin you be seen ok. **Golf** {find life go} our own]"; **and the scriptures is the penultimate** [after time life you pen] example of how to secretly hide **something** (the deepest historical meanings of life) in plain sight. In conclusion, I believe because of our relative placement in God's purposed reality, everything that can be thought of has already been thought of. Everything that we as humans can learn to think of is merely an afterthought in God's preordained purpose.

THE END [done in wee-wee thought]

EPILOGUE

During my development of this treatise, I stumbled onto several anagrams that are apropos to these discussions. I trust that you will find them useful regarding the linguistic apparatus that I have outlined here.

Residue Anagrams [side game already ways you answer]

Talks = stalk	Pride = pried	Low = owl
Priest = esprit	Read = dear = dare	Tow = two
Liar = rail	Male = meal = lame	Kids = skid
Loop = pool	Odor = door	Real = Earl
Bra = bar	Cures = curse	Smile = Miles
Hose = hoes = shoe	Laid = dial	Denial = Daniel
Seal = sale	Was = saw	Use = sue
Heir = hire	Flow = fowl = wolf	Santa = Satan
Dealing = leading	Secure = rescue	Heat = hate

Hits = shit   Mood = doom   Ends = send

Gear = rage   Runt = turn   And = Dan

Brain = Brian   Car = arc   Ain't = anti

Smite = times   Steal = least   Sword = words

Said = aids   Angel = angle = glean   Master = stream

Ages = sage   Sodom = dooms   Stare = tears

Respect = specter   Raw = war   minute = minute

Devil = lived   Ear = are = era   slave = laves

Present = serpent   Tire = tier   team = meat

Lead = deal   Tea = eat = ate   shape = phase = heaps

Live = evil   Taxes = Texas   mars = arms

Wines = swine   Arts = star   space = scape = paces

Add = Dad   Lewd = weld   bare = bear

Gum = mug   Takes = stake = steak   thin = hint

Tar = art = rat   Ways = sway   spam = maps

Made = dame   Detail = tailed   amen = mean

Ship = hips   Ours = sour   selah - heals

REFERENCES

Heidegger, Martin. <u>On the Way to Language</u>, New York: HarperCollins Publishers, 1982.

<u>Being and Time</u>, Albany: State University of New York Press, 1996.

Johnson, Larry Odell. <u>The Mind Factory: The ability to cipher information is a secret of the Lexicon</u>, USA: Writers' Branding, 2021.

Johnson, Larry Odell. I <u>Am a Key: Clarifying some elements of my first book</u>, USA: Writers' Branding, 2021.

Johnson, Larry Odell. <u>A thirteen-volume hardback set of my unpublished personal research notes on my study of language.</u>

Samantha-Laughton, Dr. Majir. <u>Punk Science: Inside the mind of God</u>, Washington, USA: O Books, 2006.

www.ingramcontent.com/pod-product-compliance
Lightning Source LLC
Chambersburg PA
CBHW020321130626
46549CB00003B/961